**Cover:** A Yanomami woman, decked out in her party best for a feast, has adorned her face with black and rose dyes and inserted three sticks round her bottom lip. In the background photograph, a group of children make their way across the unroofed central plaza of one of the circular buildings in which the Indian communities live.

**Front end-paper:** The circle on this outline map of the world encompasses the frontier areas of Venezuela and Brazil where some 300 separate groups of Yanomami live within the uncharted depths of the rain forest. Their lands are cut by many rivers, which the Indians must ford or cross by bridges made of slippery poles and ropes of liana.

---

**Peoples of the Wild Series**

---

This volume is one in a series that undertakes to record the unique lifestyles of remote peoples who have not yet yielded to the encroaching pressures of the modern world.

---

PLANET EARTH
PEOPLES OF THE WILD
THE EPIC OF FLIGHT
THE SEAFARERS
WORLD WAR II
THE GOOD COOK
THE TIME-LIFE ENCYCLOPAEDIA
OF GARDENING
HUMAN BEHAVIOUR
THE GREAT CITIES
THE ART OF SEWING
THE OLD WEST
THE WORLD'S WILD PLACES
THE EMERGENCE OF MAN
LIFE LIBRARY OF PHOTOGRAPHY
THIS FABULOUS CENTURY
TIME-LIFE LIBRARY OF ART
FOODS OF THE WORLD
GREAT AGES OF MAN
LIFE SCIENCE LIBRARY
LIFE NATURE LIBRARY
YOUNG READERS LIBRARY
LIFE WORLD LIBRARY
THE TIME-LIFE BOOK OF BOATING
TECHNIQUES OF PHOTOGRAPHY
LIFE AT WAR
LIFE GOES TO THE MOVIES
BEST OF LIFE

# Aborigines of the Amazon Rain Forest
## The Yanomami

by Robin Hanbury-Tenison
and the Editors of Time-Life Books
Photographs by Victor Englebert

PEOPLES OF THE WILD · TIME-LIFE BOOKS · AMSTERDAM

TIME-LIFE BOOKS

*European Editor:* Kit van Tulleken
*Design Director:* Louis Klein
*Photography Director:* Pamela Marke
*Planning Director:* Alan Lothian
*Chief of Research:* Vanessa Kramer
*Chief Sub-Editor:* Ilse Gray

PEOPLES OF THE WILD
*Series Editor:* Gillian Boucher
*Head Researcher:* Jackie Matthews
*Picture Editor:* Jeanne Griffiths
*Series Designer:* Rick Bowring
*Series Co-ordinators:* Belinda Stewart Cox, Elizabeth Jones

Editorial Staff for *Aborigines of the Amazon Rain Forest*
*Text Editor:* Tony Allan
*Staff Writer:* Eluned James
*Researcher:* Eleanor Lines
*Sub-Editors:* Charles Boyle, Sally Rowland
*Proofreader:* Judith Heaton
*Design Assistant:* Paul Reeves

Editorial Production
*Chief:* Ellen Brush
*Quality Control:* Douglas Whitworth
*Traffic Co-ordinators:* Jane Lillicrap, Linda Mallett
*Picture Co-ordinator:* Rebecca Read
*Art Department:* Janet Matthew
*Editorial Department:* Debra Lelliott, Sylvia Osborne

*Time-Life Correspondents:* Maria Vincenza Aloisi and Joséphine du Brusle, Paris

Published by Time-Life Books B.V., Ottho Heldringstraat 5, 1066 AZ Amsterdam.

ISBN 7054 0707 1

TIME-LIFE is a trademark of Time Incorporated U.S.A.

# Contents

### The Author

Robin Hanbury-Tenison, O.B.E., a distinguished explorer and author, was born in England in 1936. In 1958 he made the first land crossing of South America at its widest point. Since then he has travelled widely throughout the continent, visiting in the course of his travels some 45 Indian groups. Outside America, he led the Royal Geographical Society expedition to the Mulu region of Sarawak in 1977. He is the Chairman of Survival International, the charity that helps tribal people to protect their rights.

### The Photographer

Victor Englebert is a Belgian-born photojournalist who lived in Zaire, Canada and the United States before settling in Colombia in 1972. He has travelled extensively off the beaten track in Africa, Asia and South America, and his work has appeared in many international publications. He has also written several books for children.

### The Volume Consultant

Bruce Albert, a member of the Laboratoire d'Ethnologie et de Sociologie Comparative at the University of Paris X—Nanterre, was born in Morocco of French parents in 1952. He first visited northern Brazil in 1975 and has since spent more than two years doing field research among the Yanomami. He is the co-author of a National Park project which, with the aid of worldwide publicity from Survival International, aims to protect the Yanomami homelands from economic exploitation.

### The Series Consultant

Malcolm McLeod, Keeper of Ethnography at the British Museum, was born in Edinburgh. After studying History and Social Anthropology at Oxford, he undertook research in Africa, concentrating on the Asante region and other areas of Ghana. He has taught in the Sociology Department of the University of Ghana and at Cambridge. His book *The Asante* was published in 1981.

# Introduction

The land around the Guyana Shield massif on the border between Brazil and Venezuela, where the Yanomami Indians live, is one of the least-known regions on earth. Straddling the watershed between the Amazon and Orinoco river basins, it is covered by dense rain forest that is itself a formidable barrier to penetration by outsiders. In addition, the rivers that elsewhere in the area provide access to boats are here blocked by rapids.

In this remote forest fastness, the Yanomami are cut off by more than geography alone. Culturally and linguistically, they are quite distinct from all the surrounding peoples—a fact that has led anthropologists to speculate that they may be descendants of one of the earliest migrations into South America, thought to have taken place in the depths of pre-history more than 20,000 years ago. For the vast majority of the ensuing centuries, they had no contact with the outside world, and today they remain the largest group of generally isolated Indians in the Americas.

This ancient and remote people seemed promising material for the *Peoples of the Wild* series, but at first it was doubtful whether an expedition could be successfully mounted in their territory. The logistical difficulties of taking a team into the rain forest were considerable, and the problem of communication with the Indians, who speak only their own complex and little-known language, was apparently insurmountable. Additional research, however, brought to light one man who, through his previous contacts with the Yanomami of Brazil and his knowledge of their language, could make such a trip possible. He was Bruce Albert, a young French anthropologist who had lived with the Indians for more than two years. He willingly agreed to accompany Colombian-based photographer Victor Englebert and author Robin Hanbury-Tenison, an explorer well known for his work in defending the interests of threatened peoples.

The three men spent six weeks in the company of a community of Yanomami living beside the Toototobi river on the Brazilian side of the border. They integrated themselves into the daily life of the group, tracking through the forest with hunters in search of game, sharing their food and participating in a busy round of feasts. The result of their experience is an intimate portrait of one of the world's least familiar peoples, explaining with sympathy and comprehension a way of life that has remained largely unchanged for thousands of years.

**The Editors**

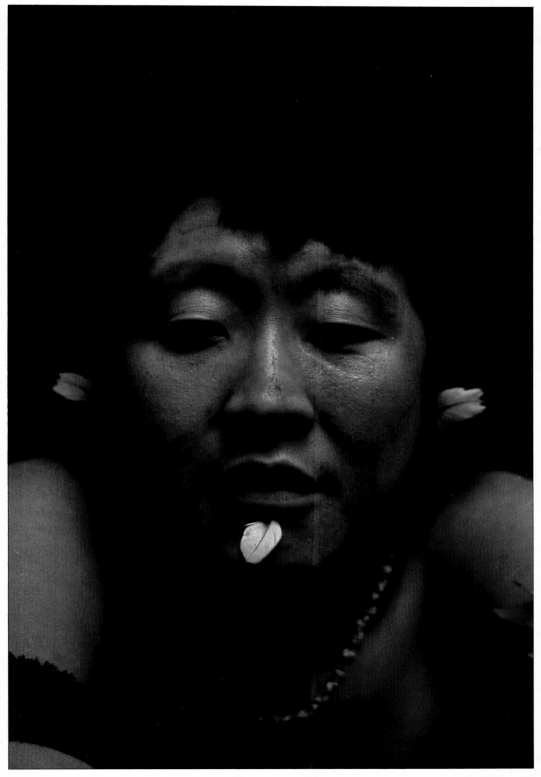

# One | A Clearing in the Forest

My first encounter with a community of Yanomami Indians was not propitious. It was 1968, and I was travelling with an ethnobotanist friend up the Ocamo, a Venezuelan tributary of the Orinoco river, searching for rare botanic specimens. We knew that some Yanomami who had little contact with outsiders lived along the Ocamo and we hoped to meet them. First, however, we stopped at a mission post by the tributary's mouth, and there we met a few of the Indians—atypical Yanomami who, through the presence of the missionaries, had become familiar with white men. Two of these Spanish-speaking Yanomami offered to serve as our guides.

For five or six hours we travelled upstream through virgin forest in a long-boat powered by an outboard motor. Several times our progress was impeded by rapids, which we managed to navigate through the skill of our guides. Elsewhere the river was calm and there was something dreamlike about the unbroken vista of forest that stretched ahead on both banks.

Then, suddenly, the tree cover fell away, and out of the forest a wall of thatched palm, like the side of some vast haystack, rose a few feet back from the river. It was my first sight of a yano—the huge circular dwelling in which whole communities of Yanomami live. With shouts and cries, Indians naked but for cotton waistbands emerged from gaps in the yano's walls and ran to meet us at the river bank. Their mood was excited but friendly, and although we halted only long enough to take on a guide who could help us to locate the botanic specimens we sought, we were given to understand that we would be welcome if we wished to spend the night as their guests. Promising to return before dusk, we set off again up the river.

A few miles upstream we located the plant we were seeking—a tree whose seeds are used in the making of the hallucinogenic drug *yopo*—and took some leaf samples. Having duly completed our botanic work, we returned to the canoe and set off back to the yano. It was already late in the afternoon. Less than an hour's daylight remained by the time we again saw the elegant

curve of the thatched walls rising among the trees, and we were congratulating ourselves on our wisdom in accepting the hospitality of the yano's inhabitants rather than facing the voyage back over the rapids in the dark. Yet even before our boat touched the shore, we knew that something was wrong. Before, the Yanomami had come out to greet us; now an eerie silence enclosed the yano. Sensing danger, our guides suggested that we change our plans and continue downriver, but I was eager to see more of this virtually unknown community and rashly insisted on entering the building.

Passing through one of the low entrances of the compound's wall, I found myself standing on the edge of a large, open space. The rim of the enclosure was shaded by a roof of thatch, beneath which the Indians had slung their hammocks and arrayed their possessions. The centre of the yano was a circular clearing or plaza, about 150 feet across, with a floor of beaten earth. In its midpoint, a fire was burning. Behind the fire, the men of the yano, perhaps 40 in all, were lined up facing me. Each man brandished a six-foot hunting bow and arrows that were even longer, some of them half as tall again as the men who held them. The welcoming smiles and gestures of the morning were gone; now the air was vibrant with menace.

I had brought a camera with me, and almost automatically I raised it to photograph the scene. Before I could release the shutter, I was seized from behind by one of the mission guides, who had come with me into the yano. Muttering angrily, he pulled me towards the entrance. As he was speaking, a shout went up from the centre of the clearing and the warriors ran towards us, shaking their weapons above their heads. I needed no additional encouragement to hurry back to the boat. The Indians followed us out of the yano, reaching the bank of the river as we pulled out into midcurrent. One or two arrows were loosed after the boat, but they sailed high above our heads, intended no doubt as a warning rather than as a serious threat to our lives. Even so, we passed some nervous moments before the canoe had travelled out of range of the Indians' powerful bows. Badly shaken by the experience, we retreated downstream to spend the night at the mission.

In retrospect, the sight of the warriors lined up inside the yano that afternoon now seems to me to typify the image that outsiders have traditionally had of the Yanomami. Neighbouring Indian peoples have long viewed them as dangerous warriors, a reputation that became standard among almost all early travellers to the area. This view of the Yanomami was revived recently by an anthropological study which christened them "the fierce people".

It is certainly true, as I discovered that day, that their behaviour can seem fierce. But the appearance of fierceness is often deceptive. The Yanomami prize the warrior virtues and often talk of raiding, thereby showing off their courage and contempt for death; but most of the time such verbal bravado is a substitute for physical violence. Other anthropologists who have lived with the tribe in recent years report that much that seems warlike in the Indians' conduct is in fact intended as a deterrent show of force to discourage aggression on the part of others.

My own experience on the Ocamo river was, as I subsequently learnt, an example of this process. The mission post later received word that a young girl had died in the interim between our first and second visits. The fire burning on our return to the yano had been a funeral pyre. What the cause of the girl's death was, I do not know; but in the highly charged situation following her demise, our return was extremely unpropitious. Sensing a further threat in our presence, the Indians had decided to scare us away.

The incident was much on my mind when I returned to Yanomami territory, for it illustrated just how easy it is for foreigners to misunderstand the motives of this remote and self-sufficient people. Before my return, I had studied all the accounts I could find of the Yanomami lifestyle, and discovered little in them to justify the reputation that the tribe had acquired in the outside world. What I learnt was that, in the inaccessible, forested hills that span the border between Brazil and Venezuela, the Yanomami have supported themselves for centuries by a combination of horticulture, in gardens cleared by slash-and-burn techniques, and by hunting, gathering and some fishing. They live in closely knit communities, yet their lifestyle is seminomadic. For their homes are abandoned every few years, when game becomes scarce in the neighbourhood and land suitable for gardening becomes hard to find. Then the entire population will move to a new yano, built elsewhere in their territory. But the villagers will continue to revisit their old haunts to gather produce growing untended in long-abandoned gardens— particularly the fruit of the peach-palm tree, which does not grow in the wild but remains fertile in formerly cultivated sites for several decades.

From the descriptions that I read of gardening, hunting and gathering in the forest, and of the intense social life in the yano, I carried away an impression of a harmonious and rewarding way of life. Yet stories of the supposed savagery of the Indians continued to appear. I had seen commentaries in respected Western periodicals that had questioned whether the Yanomami could even be considered as fully human. Popular newspapers had been

Afternoon sunlight glints on the Toototobi river and the thatched roofs of two yanos— the circular dwellings in which Yanomami communities live—set amid dense rain forest near Brazil's border with Venezuela.

even more harsh; a widely circulated American weekly had pilloried them as "the world's most vicious people". The discrepancy between the reports I had read of a friendly and peaceful way of life and the scaremongering press stories fascinated me. I set off on the expedition to their lands intent on discovering how the paradox could be resolved.

I was fortunate to be travelling in the company of a man well qualified to explain the people to me. Bruce Albert, a French anthropologist, had already spent more than two years in the company of a neighbouring Yanomami group, and was known to several individuals in the yano in which we would stay. Besides being widely conversant with their manners and customs, he was also fluent in the Yanomami language.

With photographer Victor Engelbert, we planned to fly from Boa Vista, capital of the federal territory of Roraima, Brazil's northernmost province, to the community of Toototobi, just 70 miles from the Venezuelan border. A Protestant mission post had been established nearby and beside the mission huts a small airstrip had been cleared in the forest. We set off on the 200-mile flight in a plane owned and operated by the Asa de Socorro—"Wing of Help"—an air service that is the principal means of communication, radio apart, with the missionary stations of northern Brazil.

For half an hour the plane passed over a yellow savannah scattered with dried-up ponds, a dull and largely lifeless zone relieved only occasionally by thin ribbons of palm trees marking the course of rivers that run during the rainy season. This stretch of scrubland to the west of Boa Vista has been infertile since time immemorial; geographers are still undecided whether its sterility is the result of very ancient local climatic conditions or of land clearance in the remote and unrecorded past. For me, it stood as an ominous reminder of what happens to the rain forest when the tree cover is stripped away. Deprived of the protection that the foliage affords, the soil erodes under the impact of periodic heavy rains until it can support only the most miserable scraps of vegetation.

Abruptly, the land below us began to change. First we saw a thin line of trees, then a broad river, the Mucajai. Beyond, on the river's western bank, the rain forest began. It stretched before us, apparently endless in its immensity, like some vast green carpet, dotted sporadically with a vivid splash of red or yellow where the tops of flowering trees broke the monotony of the verdure. From time to time, looking down on the greenery, I noticed a break where a river cut a meandering line, and at one point the forest fell away to reveal a cluster of isolated rock ridges rising too steeply for even the tenacious Amazonian vegetation to take a hold.

After we had flown for almost an hour, the contours of the carpet beneath us became less even. The forest floor was wrinkled, its surface broken by small hills. On the horizon I could clearly make out mountains between 2,500 and 5,000 feet high. These were the peaks of the Parima and Urucuzeiro massifs, outcrops of the Guyana Shield range that runs along the Venezuelan border. They mark the heartland of the Yanomami. I knew that we must be

Inside a yano, a group of women—one with
a baby on her back—cross the central plaza
on their way to collect water from the nearby
river. Beneath the building's circular roof,
screens made from woven palm fronds hang
between support poles to provide shade.

getting close to Toototobi, which lies at 600 feet—a relatively low altitude for this slope-dwelling people—on the southern, Brazilian side of the range.

Sure enough, as I gazed downwards from the plane's window, I soon spotted a yellow, doughnut-shaped structure set into an irregularly shaped clearing in the forest. It was the thatched roof of a yano. Then I saw another, maybe a mile away across a river, and a third some distance to the north. Close to each building were clearings carpeted with low vegetation, which I recognized as the gardens in which the Indians grow their crops.

The aircraft came in to land on a simple grass strip that traversed so steep a hump that from the near end of the runway the farther extremity was out of sight. Stepping out of the plane, we found ourselves in a clearing surrounded on all sides by impenetrable scrub, a secondary vegetation that had grown up where the tree cover had at some stage been burnt away. A patch of cane more than twice the height of a man grew at one end of the runway; I was later to learn that the Indians used the long, firm stalks for making arrows. A path led eastwards through a maze of peach palms and tangled undergrowth in the direction of the mission huts.

The sun beat down on us and the heat was sweltering. The only building in sight was a simple shelter, with a roof of palm fronds supported on four wooden poles. Turning instinctively to its promise of shade, we saw beneath it the post's two missionaries—one of whom was departing on leave on the plane that had brought us—and maybe 50 or 60 Yanomami.

The first thing that I noticed about the Indians was their small stature. Few of the men were more than five feet tall, and the women were on average six inches shorter. The men were almost totally naked, wearing only cotton waistbands, to which each man had attached the prepuce of his penis. This apparently purposeless custom, not unknown among other Amerindian groups, is extremely important in the Yanomami code of correct behaviour. Any man appearing in public with his waistband incorrectly adjusted would feel as ill at ease as a Westerner forced to appear in company without his clothes. Otherwise, the men's only decoration was a faint blush of *urucu*, a red vegetable dye used for body painting by most of the Amazonian tribes.

Like the men, the women wore waistbands; in addition, they had miniature cotton aprons with a fringe of thick cotton threads about three inches long. These threads were stained red with *urucu*, and some of the women had interspersed them with brightly coloured toucan feathers and with shells and hollow nuts designed to jangle as they walked. In addition, they all wore decorative, red-dyed armbands, into which they had inserted feathers and leaves chosen for their fragrance. The women's bodies were stained a darker shade of red than the men's, though the colour of the dye blended so naturally into the warm tone of their skin that the effect was one of nature enhanced, not disguised. Men and women alike had thick black hair, cut uniformly in a circular, "pudding basin" style.

The Indians were talking animatedly among themselves, and the sound of their voices impressed me even though I could not understand the words. They spoke in a rapid, staccato chatter. Some displayed great vocal agility in

Her ears and arms adorned with leaves, a girl washes herself in the waters of the Toototobi river. The long sliver of wood that she wears through her nose and the plant stems that pierce her lower lip are both typical decorations for Yanomami women.

AIRSTRIP

MISSION BUILDINGS

Fialho's yano

Toototobi yano

Plinio's yano

Toototobi River

BRAZIL

N

## Riverside Settlements

The homeland of the Yanomami Indians lies between the Orinoco and Amazon basins, athwart the boundary of Venezuela and Brazil. Their territory covers more than 60,000 square miles of rain forest, broken by streams flowing down from the Guyana Shield mountains.

The 200 or so Yanomami of the Toototobi river district live deep within this vast expanse on the Brazilian side of the frontier (inset map). Near the Toototobi yano itself are mission buildings and an airstrip built in 1962 by a Protestant evangelical organization. To the north are two yanos established by Indians originally from the Toototobi group. The nearest of the two, whose headman is Fialho, is about 20 minutes' walk away across the river. The second, under the aegis of Plinio, lies five miles beyond.

Alongside each homestead, the Yanomami fell and burn trees to create gardens where they grow staples such as manioc and plantain. All around, the boundless forest offers a rich variety of fruits and game. In addition, isolated ponds, created when the river level drops in the drier months from October to March, provide fishing grounds.

the way in which they would draw out a vowel sound to lend emphasis to a point, or emit a long groan, punctuated by a clicking of the tongue, to express irritation. Once or twice a man would burst into laughter, a loud guffaw ending on a sustained rising note that became a cry of pure joy.

I observed the Indians at my leisure in the time that it took the departing missionary to load his family and luggage on to the aircraft. Finally all was ready; the plane teetered down the treacherous airstrip, rose high above the trees and was gone. In the company of the remaining missionary—a polite Englishman named Tony Poulson who asked me if I knew Bournemouth, his home town—Bruce, Victor and I made our way with our baggage along the path that linked the airstrip to the mission buildings, 10 minutes' walk away.

The path lay through a former garden that was slowly reverting to forest. It is a curious feature of the Amazon basin that areas of secondary vegetation are much more overgrown at ground level than the forest itself. Land that has once been cleared and has then returned to its natural state, such as that which we were passing through, is tangled and matted with waist-high grasses and scrub. In areas of virgin woodland, however, where the trees rise as high as 200 feet, most of the plant life is to be found overhead. Below the forest canopy itself, tangles of liana reach down past clusters of epiphytes—high-growing plants that sprout from every available crevice on the massive tree trunks—to the struggling saplings awaiting their chance to reach the sky. The forest floor is surprisingly free of vegetation because little direct sunlight reaches it to encourage growth. It is a green, damp, warm, apparently tranquil world, where all light is muted and bright colours are rare. The permanent shade is broken infrequently by a stray shaft of sunlight that dapples the dead leaves and rotting logs that cover the earth, forming a rich humus that in turn nourishes new growths starting their search for the sun.

Emerging from the undergrowth, we found ourselves suddenly in a bright clearing containing five rectangular huts, each made of wattle and daub and roofed with thatch. These were the mission buildings. Each one was shaded by fruit trees and surrounded by a patch of new-mown lawn—a surrealistic touch amid the luxuriant vegetation of the rain forest.

Behind the mission huts, a thin belt of forest concealed the Toototobi river. Hot and tired as Victor and I were after our journey, the first thing we wanted to do was to go for a swim. Bruce, meanwhile, went towards the yano to re-establish contact with his old friends and warn them that two strangers would soon appear in their midst.

Leaving our equipment in the clearing, Victor and I made our way down a track to a point where a sandy beach stretched for 20 yards or so along the water's edge. Wide and slow-flowing, the brown stream cut silently through the trees as it pursued its course from a source in the Urucuzeiro highlands to the point 50 miles to the south of Toototobi where it joined the Demini river. The Demini in its turn would carry its waters to the Rio Negro, the mightiest of the Amazon's 1,100 tributaries. We had soon stripped off our clothing and waded out into the current. At its deepest, the water barely reached our thighs, for we had arrived in early April, near the end of the six-

Crouching on an unfinished section of the yano's roof above the hearth where he and his family live, Mateus, who played host to the members of the Time-Life expedition, concentrates on lashing two poles together with strands of liana. Like all the Yanomami living at Toototobi, he bears a Christian name given to him by local missionaries in addition to his own Indian name.

month dry season. One month later, its depth would have increased fourfold.

We lay back in the water and let the river envelop us. A few bird cries, among them the rattle of the Amazon kingfisher and the harsh calls of a pair of blue-and-yellow macaws passing high overhead, broke the silence, and downstream we could hear the shouts and giggles of a group of Yanomami girls who were playing in the river. Otherwise peace and stillness surrounded us; but our predominant feeling was expectancy. In the deep heart of the forest, a whole world of new faces and experiences was waiting.

The community to which we were about to introduce ourselves was a small branch of a numerous people—almost certainly the largest group of Indians in all the Americas whose population is still for the most part isolated from the outside world. No accurate census of the Yanomami has ever been taken, but current estimates put their numbers between 15,000 and 20,000. The territory that they inhabit stretches over some 60,000 square miles of thickly forested country, much of it still unexplored. The border between Brazil and Venezuela runs through the very heart of their land, following the watershed between the Amazon and Orinoco river basins. This area has never been fully surveyed, however, and topographical information on even the most up-to-date maps is given as "incomplete".

The people who range over this remote expanse are in many ways unique. Some experts think that their history stretches back further than that of almost any other people in the Americas. Most if not all American aboriginals are generally agreed to have arrived from Asia at a time in the remote past when what is now the Bering Strait was covered by a land bridge linking Siberia and Alaska. Opinions are constantly changing as to when this may have happened, the tendency being for new evidence to push the date back. The earliest carbon-14-dated archaeological sites for North America are now about 40,000 years old; the figure for South America is 20,000 years.

The evidence for the Yanomami's special position among South American groups is genetic. All other Amerindians so far tested have been found to possess in varying degrees a certain gene, known as the Diego factor, found only in the blood of Mongoloid peoples. The Yanomami, however, are Diego negative. This fact has persuaded some geneticists that the Yanomami represent the descendants of a relatively small group who have remained completely isolated in the same area for a very long time.

Linguistic research too seems to support this hypothesis. Studies conducted so far have revealed two important points: first, that the Yanomami have no linguistic affinity with neighbouring peoples, and secondly that their language group consists of four distinct languages, all mutually intelligible. It is generally accepted that such diversification of an original mother tongue is a process requiring many thousands of years. It is therefore possible to believe that the Yanomami may be the sole remnants of the earliest migrations into South America many thousands of years ago.

Several theories have been advanced to explain what it was that brought the Yanomami to the sheltered patch of country where they now live. Some anthropologists have suggested that, in the unimaginably distant past, they may have hunted now-extinct animals such as mastodons, armadillo-like glyptodons, giant sloths and even wild American horses; having chased the animals into these remote hide-outs, they decided to stay. Another theory holds that they may once have been a farming people cultivating the relatively rich-soiled lowlands of the Amazon Basin, but were pushed northwards under pressure from later immigrant groups and forced to adopt a more nomadic lifestyle in the higher lands of the Guyana Shield.

Whatever the truth may be—and for want of any substantial archaeological evidence it is almost impossible to prove any theory—the Yanomami were extraordinarily fortunate in their choice of territory. Dwelling on the watershed between the Amazon and Orinoco river basins, they have benefited from the dual protection of the dense rain forest and the broken terrain. Elsewhere, the tributaries that feed the Orinoco and the Amazon have provided access routes for outsiders, but the rivers in the Guyana Shield region are small and interrupted by rapids. This important geographical defence has in the past saved the Yanomami from the fate of many other South American Indian peoples, whose lands lay on the routes used by such invaders as the Arawaks and the Caribs. In the course of their northward migrations, these powerful Indian groups, who at one time or another occupied all the land from the middle Amazon through the Guyanas and the Caribbean to Florida, tended to follow the major navigable rivers or to travel by sea, conquering or assimilating other peoples as they went. Although they settled all around the mountains, they were not tempted to penetrate the forest fastnesses the Yanomami had chosen as their home.

With the arrival of European invaders from the Old World, following Christopher Columbus's voyage of 1492, came new dangers to the Indian population of South America. Catastrophic epidemics of imported diseases previously unknown on the continent wiped out entire Amerindian peoples who lacked any resistance to them. These epidemics, too, failed to reach the Yanomami because of their geographic isolation. Even the energetic efforts made to discover Manoa, the legendary city of gold believed by 17th-century adventurers to lie on a lake somewhere in the Parima highlands, and later Portuguese expeditions in search of Indian slaves, left the Yanomami undisturbed. The explorers took more convenient routes along the major river systems in search of their goals.

The first incursions into what is now Yanomami territory were made by the Portuguese colonizers of Brazil and the Spaniards who had settled Venezuela. These intrusions did not occur until the latter half of the 18th century, nearly 300 years after the first arrival of Europeans on the continent. Spanish soldiers reconnoitering the upper reaches of the Orinoco entered the fringes of the Yanomami's land in 1760. The first Portuguese to enter present-day Brazilian Yanomami country were a border commission who in 1787 had the task of surveying the border with the Spanish territories. Fortunately for the Yanomami, however, the reputation for ferocity they enjoyed among the Indians from other peoples who acted as guides for the intruders was so

Three men on their way to a feast at a nearby yano use a banana leaf to shelter themselves from a shower. The two leading men are wearing their gourd drinking bowls over their heads to leave their hands free and provide extra protection from the rain.

formidable that no attempt to make contact with them was even considered.

The Yanomami's supposed hostility, combined with the inhospitableness of the terrain, continued to discourage explorers of the northern Amazon Basin from any sustained contact for a further 150 years. During this time, the Yanomami experienced a golden age, during which their population and territory expanded considerably. The few travellers who did find their way into their lands did their best to avoid the natives. It was not until the late 1920s that the Yanomami were subjected to major intrusions, when gatherers of latex found their way to the area. At first the Indians were totally bemused by the newcomers. An old Yanomami man once described to Bruce the first impression the strangers made on the group with which he was then living. Finding bootprints by the rivers, the Indians had asked themselves what toeless creature could have left them; and when they saw the men themselves, they were intrigued above all by their clothes, which they took for second skins that the possessors could slough at will.

These first invaders were followed by prospectors in search of valuable minerals, and hunters seeking jaguar and ocelot skins. With them, inevitably, they brought diseases to which the Yanomami had never acquired biological resistance: epidemics of measles, whooping cough and influenza which substantially decreased the population in some areas. The Indians retaliated by attacking the outsiders and eventually succeeded in discouraging the gatherers from penetrating their territory.

One remarkable encounter that was to generate a great deal of unfavourable publicity for the Yanomami took place in 1937, when the 11-year-old daughter of a Brazilian rubber gatherer was kidnapped by the Indians. She and her family had been travelling up the Dimiti river by canoe when they were attacked; the rest of the family escaped. The girl lived with her captors for 22 years, bearing four sons to two different husbands. Having no family of her own to turn to for protection, and also being burdened with the low status of a foreigner, she was always at a disadvantage, and was finally taken back to the outside world with her sons by her second Yanomami husband. The published description of her life with the Indians, recorded and edited by an Italian doctor, depicted the tenderness and richness of their lives but, to dramatize the story, tended to emphasize less attractive traits such as infanticide and inter-group raiding. Predictably, these aspects received more attention than the clues she gave to the sophistication of Yanomami culture.

The capture of this girl was a rarity; generally it was the Yanomami who were the victims in their encounters with outsiders. I learnt the story of one such meeting from a first-hand witness during the course of my visit. One of the older Indians in the group with which we were staying told me of an event that occurred in the late 1950s, when the Toototobi community were living a day's journey north of their present site.

A group of prospectors arrived unannounced at the Indians' yano, and one of them demanded that a woman be provided for him. The request was not unfamiliar to the Indians, who had had occasional contact with such bands of wandering, ruffianly adventurers before; their habit was to comply if possible with such demands, for they feared hostile sorcery from the newcomers if they failed to do so. A widow was persuaded unwillingly to accompany the intruders, but during the night she escaped and ran back to the yano.

The next morning the strangers had gone. Shortly afterwards the Indians started to fall sick in large numbers. Many of them died until, my friend said, "there were corpses lying everywhere". The Indians correctly attributed this epidemic to the arrival of the prospectors. However, they took it to be the result of sorcery, provoked by the visitors' anger at the woman's flight, rather than measles, as was probably the case. The Indians wished to revenge themselves upon the prospectors for the harm they had caused, but were too ill to follow them; and by that time, in any case, they were far away.

Most of the Yanomami's brushes with the outside world took the form of incidents of this unsavoury kind until sustained contact was finally established by Christian missionaries attached to a Protestant, American-based evangelical organization called the New Tribes Mission. Their earliest activities were centred on the Upper Orinoco in Venezuela, where a base was set up in 1947. The Toototobi mission, where we were staying, dated from 1962 and was the first station to be founded on Brazilian soil. A few Catholic missionaries are also now working in Yanomami territory in both Brazil and Venezuela. In some areas, the missionaries have already had a substantial disruptive impact on the Indians' lifestyle and complex beliefs, which centre

Bedecked with beads and shoots of palm, a woman and two young girls pause in a forest clearing to groom themselves and remove lice from one another's hair. Lice are one of the minor irritations of Yanomami life, and delousing is a daily chore. To kill them, the Indians crush them between their teeth.

on a world of spirits that can be contacted by shamans credited with healing powers under the influence of hallucinogens. At Toototobi, however, the proselytizers' activities have been limited by their isolation, and their success in altering the behaviour of the Indians has been minimal.

Contact with other outsiders has increased over the past decades, and since 1959 at least eight separate measles epidemics have cost the lives of several hundred Yanomami throughout their territory. In the mid-1970s, a branch of the projected Trans-Amazon Highway was constructed through the southern part of their lands, plans were laid to develop millions of acres of their eastern territory, and 500 settlers swarmed into the Parima Massif, near the centre of the Yanomami lands, following the discovery of surface deposits of tin; they were expelled after more than a year, under government legislation to protect the Indians' land. No sooner had they left, however, than gold was found and a fresh wave of several thousand migrants started to penetrate the extreme east of the Yanomami homeland.

Despite the recent encroachments, contact with foreigners is still much less important to most of the Indians than encounters with other Yanomami. It sometimes seems hard to understand how the people have remained culturally homogeneous in spite of the vast areas over which its members are scattered. The answer seems to lie in the multitude of visits among different yanos. Friendly neighbours are invited to feasts at which vast food surpluses are consumed at times when favoured foods such as plantain or peach palm are ripe. In addition, members of such yanos often intermarry, so that the network of kinship extends beyond the walls of each dwelling, providing opportunities for frequent family visits that increase the social interaction.

Despite such inter-yano contact, marked linguistic differences can be found within the Yanomami lands. The four major regional languages are distinguished by the way in which the speakers refer to themselves. The Toototobi community belonged to the Yanomam language group; the other groups, using different pronunciations of essentially the same word, are generally referred to as the Tsanoma, Yanam and Yanomamo, each one extending over a wide area. Like their counterparts in many developed countries, the inhabitants of each language area tend to regard those who speak differently with a certain amount of mistrust and condescension. The Yanomam-speakers of Toototobi, for instance, lived close to other Indians speaking the Yanomamo language, whom they called *shamatari*. We were later to meet some of these strangers, whose speech our friends liked to mock and whose slightly different customs they simply regarded as bad manners.

After our swim, Victor and I dried off and made our way to the yano. The first close-up view of this extraordinary building was memorable. We passed through a strip of forest that screened the yano from the mission buildings and emerged into a circular clearing. The dwelling rose in front of us to a height of 30 feet or more. Yet, despite its size, its curving wall fitted so well into its surroundings that at first it seemed a natural outgrowth rather than the cunningly constructed artefact it really was. Ducking through the low

While a couple of his playmates look on, a young boy plunges feet first from an overhanging branch into the brown waters of the Toototobi river.

gateway that served as an entrance, I found myself in the building that was to be my home for the next six weeks.

My first impression was of emptiness and space. The roofed area, covering the hammocks and hearths of the 20 family groups that made up the community, extended in a shady ring about 40 feet deep. Standing in the shadow of the overhanging roof just inside the entrance, I looked across the wide sunlit plaza as though across a bull-ring without a crowd. As my eyes adjusted to the shade of the covered area round the plaza, however, I saw that the emptiness was an illusion, and that 20 or 30 people lay in hammocks or squatted by fires, silent for a split second as they stopped to look in our direction.

As we stepped forward, the silence broke. A man's explosive laugh, brimming over with glee and good humour, rang out, shattering the expectant hush. Dogs rushed forward, barking bravely, but retired yelping when one of our hosts raised a stick at them. I became aware of a murmur of voices and children's laughter rippling around the ring; it was a sound that soon became so familiar that it merged into the background and ceased to be noticed.

Bruce was chatting with our self-appointed host in the yano, a well-built man in his mid-thirties whom he had met on field trips to villages on the Catrimani river, 100 miles to the east, where the Indian had previously lived. His Yanomami name was Irouhe—the word for a hairy, yellow caterpillar, chosen by his parents because, as a child, he had had tawny hair that stuck up in bristles. Like everyone at Toototobi, however, he had been given a second name by the missionaries who, using the language of Brazil, chose common Portuguese appellations. So it was by the name of Mateus that we generally referred to him. We found him a kind and conscientious friend, painstaking in his efforts on our behalf and infinitely tolerant of our eccentricities.

He led us to the section of the yano where he lived with his wife and four small sons. Their hammocks were slung between poles in groups of three, arranged to form equilateral triangles. Between each group a fire burned constantly, so we naturally took to describing these areas—the basic habitation units into which each yano is divided—as hearths, a term that also, by implication, covered the space between the hammocks and the yano's rear wall. This area, some six feet deep, was used for storing the firewood, pots, baskets, gourds, weapons and personal ornaments that make up the great majority of any Yanomami household's possessions.

Mateus's wife, Sonia, was waiting for us at one of the family's two hearths. She was an attractive woman, a few years younger than her husband, with lively, intelligent features. In time I was to discover that her expressive face reflected a mercurial temperament that could switch from joy to fury and back as fast as any I had ever known. Patience and kindness itself when she wished, she could also scowl darkly and shriek high-pitched abuse if either we or her children angered her, as we both frequently did. Her hearth was regularly swept clean, and her impatience at finding me in the way when there was housework to be done was to make me feel strangely at home.

After we had slung our cotton hammocks alongside those of the family, Sonia brought us a gourd of bright yellow soup made from plantains. We

Replete with banana soup, a man takes his ease in a hammock with a wad of tobacco between his lower lip and teeth. Prepared by moistening dried tobacco leaves with water, then rolling them in white ash from the family hearths, such wads are enjoyed by men, women and even some of the children.

took turns at the gourd to drink the warm, sweet liquid, sitting astride our hammocks with our bare feet firmly planted on the freshly swept mud floor. A tiny mongrel puppy of terrier-like appearance, its paws grotesquely swollen, hobbled to a new position near the embers of the fire. Only later did I learn that the feet of all the dogs, and especially the puppies, are heavily infested with the burrowing fleas known as chigoes, and that it was wise for soft-footed Europeans to wear sandals whenever possible.

Around us the life of the yano pursued its tranquil, late-afternoon course. Women lay in hammocks suckling their unweaned offspring, or sat chatting in groups around friends' hearths. Noisy bands of naked children roamed the central plaza, the boys clutching miniature bows and arrows in their hands. I noticed few men at first, but as the shadows lengthened with the approach of evening their numbers were gradually augmented by hunters returning from the forest. Those who brought game with them quickly attracted groups of inquisitive neighbours eager to inspect the day's bag.

With the coming of darkness, families gathered around their hearths to prepare for sleep. As I lay comfortably in my hammock that first night, idly scratching at the first of many flea bites on my tender, unresistant flesh, I felt myself in a kind of fairyland. A tree-rat called and was answered intermittently from down by the river, six cries followed by seven in a regular series. Owls hooted in the distance, and nightjars whistled loudly to one another with a melodic but monotonous three-tone call that swooped rapidly up the scale and then down again. Frogs and toads croaked and warbled in chorus. Always, in the background, insects chirping high in the trees filled the tropical darkness with a bell-like tinkle.

There was no moon; the only light came from the fires burning in each of the 20 hearths more or less evenly spaced around the perimeter of the yano, and from the faint glow of stars in the sky. When the flames burnt low, I had the sense of being in a vast, underground cave, silent and insulated from the world around. But every now and then a fire would flare up, as one of the women left her hammock to fan the embers. Then the curved roof of the yano was suddenly illuminated, and the sky in the centre became darker by contrast, so that it seemed like a great dome attached to the roof.

Later that night, it started to rain. I could hear the drops pattering on the thatch above my head and could see them falling in the open space in front of me, but no water found its way through the roofing. Sleepless but snug under the watertight covering of thatch, I felt a deep contentment spreading over me. For hundreds of miles in all directions, the forest surrounded me, immense, frightening and utterly different from the world I had just left. But the walls of the yano kept all the strangeness of that vast wilderness at bay. Inside, I felt sheltered not merely by the palisade of leaves around me but also by the companionship of all the other people dozing in their hammocks around the yano. It was as though the whole vast building contained a single family, of which I was, if not a member, at least a welcome guest. I was already beginning to understand something about the Yanomami.

# Cosmetics from Nature

The Yanomami are acutely conscious of their intrinsic beauty and seek constantly to enhance it: men and women alike love to paint and decorate themselves. Adolescents who are anxious to attract marriage partners take particular pride in their appearance. For special occasions such as feasts, however, all ages indulge in spectacular flights of self-adornment.

Almost all their ornaments come from nature. Flowers and leaves are picked from beside paths in the forest to accentuate pierced ears. Brilliant feathers are plucked from dead game and tucked into armbands. Women wear twigs and reeds stuck through perforations in the septum of the nose, the lower lip and the corners of the mouth. Patterns covering faces and bodies are painted with dyes derived from plants.

The commonest dye, a vivid red, comes from a flowering shrub called *urucu* that the Yanomami cultivate in their gardens. Sometimes they simply smear the oily substance that coats its seed directly on to the flesh. Otherwise, to make a pigment they can store, they heat the seeds in a pot with water to make a paste that is moulded into balls and wrapped in leaves. The ball of dye is dragged across the skin to produce bold, thick strokes; alternatively, it can be applied in finer lines with a stick.

For contrast, the Yanomami use charcoal or a black dye made from the fruit of the *genipapo* tree; they also occasionally darken the *urucu* by preparing it in pots blackened with the soot of burnt resin. While the red dye is the colour for everyday use and for feasts, they associate the darker tones with valour, so combatants in the ritual fighting that often marks the climax of feasts frequently have large areas of their bodies coloured black.

Applying the paint is a group activity, and part of the fun of dressing up. Mothers will stipple and stripe their daughters, wives will make up their husbands, and young girls will take turns to paint each other. The designs that are chosen depend on the whim of the painter and wearer. Animal markings such as the jaguar's spots are popular themes; so are abstract symbols—wavy lines, for example. A visit from a neighbouring Yanomami community who favour different patterns may well start a fashion for imitating their particular style of beautification.

His body stained with spots of red urucu dye, a Yanomami father decorates his son with bird down in preparation for a feast.

Coiffed with bird down, a youth bearing invitations to a feast poses impassively with his bow and arrows.

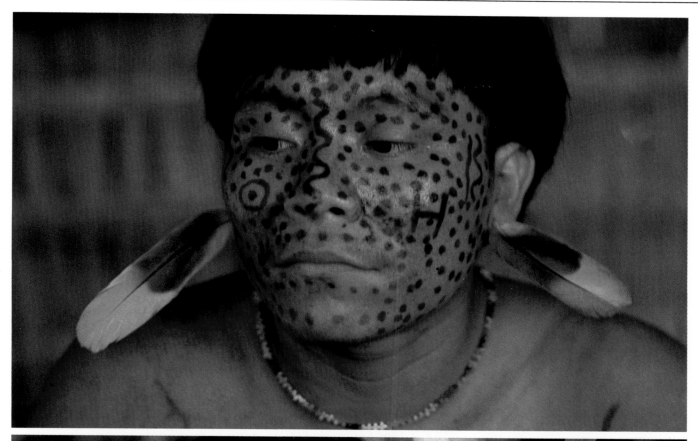

Feather decorations such as parrot earpieces (top) or an armband of turkey and macaw plumes (bottom) are vivid tributes to a hunter's skill.

With bouquets of primrose-yellow feathers
adorning her ears, a young girl sports the
characteristic, symmetrical face ornaments
of Yanomami women: reeds inserted
through holes pierced under the lower lip
and a fine sliver of wood through the nose.

With the aid of a mirror obtained through trade, a Yanomami woman paints a design of half-moons on her face.

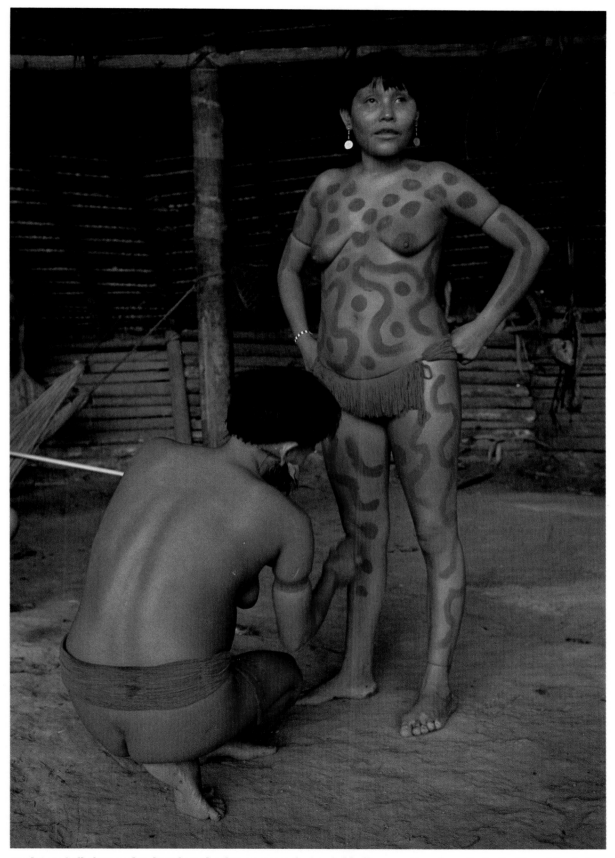

Applying a ball of urucu dye directly to the skin, a woman daubs a bold, all-over pattern down the body of her sister-in-law.

Her ears and arms bedecked with fragrant leaves, a woman concentrates intently on the task of painting a pattern on her husband's buttocks, using a stick that she has dipped in urucu. Like all Yanomami men, he wears a thin waistband of cotton.

## *Two* | **A Village under One Roof**

The yano is the theatre in which the drama of Yanomami social life unfolds. Its very shape affects the nature of the lives lived within it, for its design makes it a theatre in the round, in which actors and audiences are one and the same, and the observer is at any moment also the observed. The exact shape of the building varies from one Yanomami group to another, but almost all choose a circular plan. The Toototobi version, with its sloping roof and wide central plaza, is the most common model.

The current building was little more than a month old when I arrived, and work was still continuing on it. Although each yano is planned as a communal dwelling, it is built in separate sections, each constructed independently though concurrently by the family that will live in it. After a few weeks the framework of the completed building will already be in place. The degree of co-ordination between the builders is minimal—at most there will be one or two of the elders of the community standing in the centre of the building to direct the labours—yet the final result is invariably a satisfactory whole.

Eager to see how the structure was built, I received my first lesson early on the morrow of my arrival in the yano, when I woke up to find Mateus, our host, smiling broadly down at me from a narrow crossbeam 20 feet or so above my head. He was solicitously extending the roof of his hearth to ensure that we would not be splashed by falling rain. Although he was perched on a pole only a few inches wide, he was supporting himself without hands. It was my first glimpse of the extraordinary climbing ability and sense of balance that all Yanomami seem to possess.

The framework of the yano, which in this case was already in place, is provided by three concentric rings of hardwood poles linked by light crossbeams; a fourth, outer ring consists of small sticks rising only about four feet above the ground. The inner rings are successively taller, the innermost

being some 25 feet high. The beams are lashed into place so firmly with liana, the universal rope of the forest, that even in a strong wind the structure hardly moves. This skeleton of timber is then covered with substantial and easily lifted pieces of prefabricated thatch, formed of overlapping palm fronds tied by their stems to six-foot lengths of palmwood. A pile of these sections lay on the ground beside my hammock. Mateus's son, who was squatting nearby, tied them to a liana as they were needed. Mateus hauled them up and laid them one over another, allowing each pair to overlap by a few inches. Then he lashed them into place with more liana.

Similar palm fronds were used for the rear wall of the yano, covering the small gap between the outermost ring of roofing and the ground. At some hearths this leafy curtain was fortified by a strong palisade of wooden poles; these were usually the homes of older men who, as a result of their past experience in the days before the community moved to the relative peace of Toototobi, were more conscious of the dangers of attack, whether by enemy warriors or by hostile sorcerers. The younger families had merely a screen of leaves through which children, chickens and dogs could run.

Easily built, the yanos are also easily abandoned when they become unpleasant to inhabit as a result of the rotting of the leaf cover, the weakening of the structure through repeated buffeting by the wind, or the infestation by fleas and cockroaches reaching an unacceptable level. The average life of a building is little more than two years. The Indians may then choose to construct a new yano nearby, if there is still game to be hunted in the forest and good, productive earth in the vicinity for the gardens. Eventually, however, the resources available will diminish to a point at which a decision will be taken to build the next yano in some other part of the forest. The community will then migrate to a new site, usually less than half a dozen miles away, which has been chosen with an eye to good land for gardens, easy access to water—preferably a small stream to reduce the risk of flooding—and adequate living space to prevent infringing on the territory used by other Yanomami in the neighbourhood. In general, such moves are made every five to seven years, but special circumstances may cause the gap to be either shorter or longer. At Toototobi, for example, where the mission provided access to medicines and a certain number of imported goods, our hosts had remained sedentary in a succession of yanos for nearly two decades.

Around the yano, each family occupied an area that could vary from about five to 15 yards in length, extending over as many as four hearths. Fires burned in each occupied hearth throughout the day and night. Their smoke climbed up the sloping roof to form an invisible canopy over the central plaza that discouraged winged insects from entering the building. Within the yano's confines, I rarely saw any of the mosquitoes that were becoming numerous outside in the forests as the rains began.

Around their hearths, the Yanomami kept the relatively few possessions that their lifestyle demanded. Made from raw materials found in the forest, most could easily be replaced when they wore out. The only specialization in their craftsmanship was determined by gender; women generally made most of the domestic goods, including baskets and anything involving cotton, while the men were responsible for weapons, and especially arrows, which took more of their time than any other artefacts. Other male duties included preparing bark hammocks and repairing the structure of the yano itself. They also undertook odd jobs involving carpentry, such as putting up shelves or building tripods that could be set over the fires for smoking meat.

At the time of my visit a few articles of foreign manufacture were also to be found in the yano. The Indians had some aluminium cooking pots in addition to a few remaining clay utensils. They also owned imported machetes, knives, axes and metal fish-hooks, as well as some commercially produced hammocks and articles of clothing. Most of these goods had been obtained from other Yanomami groups who were in regular contact with the outside world. Some, however, came from the missionaries and, in return, the Indians worked in their gardens, carried water, and provided them with game.

One modern convenience upon which the Indians had become dependent was the safety match. I discovered just how necessary these were when I asked Mateus to show me how fire was made in the old days. He had seldom, if ever, had to perform the task, though he had often seen it done as a child, but he obligingly collected the necessary kit: three or four long, thin, rounded sticks and an oval block of soft wood. The wood was left to dry for several days before Mateus set about the demonstration. By rotating one of the sticks between his palms, he had soon hollowed out a small bore-hole in the block. Next, he set some pieces of dry tinder around the hole. Puffing and grunting with the effort, he twirled the stick in the hole until, after about 10 minutes, a few friction-generated sparks eventually ignited the tinder. A crowd had gathered round to watch his exertions, and there was much laughter when someone remarked that they would have a hard time of it now if they ran out

As a woman returns home with a basket of
plantains and papaya fruit that she has
gathered from her garden, a little girl
perched on her shoulders ducks under the
thatch that fringes the entrance to the yano.

of matches. Just how hard was revealed the next day when Mateus came to us to have his hand treated. On each palm there were three deep and inflamed wounds an inch or more across.

Later, Severiano, an older man, showed us how it should be done. I counted 40 twirls as, squatting with his feet on the block, he made smoke pour from the little black hole. Then, pausing for a moment, he stood up and gave 20 final, hard twirls, which had the tinder smouldering well. However, it still took all of five minutes' careful tending and gentle blowing before flames were eventually produced. Severiano suffered no problems with his hands because, he told us, his palms had become hardened by making fire to smoke out bees when he was much younger.

With the exception of matches and steel tools, however, most of the imported goods could still be dispensed with, or replaced by native artefacts made with materials found easily in the surrounding forest. In 1977, I was told in proof of this, a yano in the Catrimani area burnt down, after an old woman had set burning leaves under the skirt of the building to drive out fleas. Almost everything was destroyed. Yet the inhabitants treated the destruction of all their possessions as merely a disruption, not a catastrophe. They built temporary shelters to house themselves while the yano was rebuilt, and within a short time all the necessary accoutrements of life had been refashioned. The continuity of their lives was barely interrupted. It is hard for a Westerner, dependent upon manufactured commodities, to appreciate the sense of security and self-confidence that comes from knowing that most of the things one possesses can be replaced in a matter of hours.

Along with matches, the most treasured imports were the machetes and axes, obtained through trade, which greatly simplified the task of gardening. A garden is an essential adjunct of every yano, for its produce provides much of the vegetable content of the inhabitants' diets, and clearing and tending it is a regular daily task.

One of the few times when the Yanomami labour communally is during the preparation of a new garden, a lengthy process that may stretch over six months or more. The first job is to find a suitable site, with fertile soil on flat terrain beyond the reach of floodwater. The next task is to cut down the saplings, shrubs and lianas which cloak the ground between the principal forest trees. Then the trees themselves must be felled. The normal time for this task is in October or November, at the beginning of the dry season. Before the advent of metal implements it was an extremely laborious process. Forest giants were burnt down; smaller trees were cleared with tomahawk-like stone axes. Now, however, even the largest trees are cut down with steel axes, which do the job in less than half the time required with stone tools.

Once all the trees have been cleared, the detritus is left to desiccate—which may mean waiting until January or February, when the dry season is well under way. When it is completely combustible, fires are started; they have the triple effect of clearing the land, killing off unwanted seeds and parasitic insects, and producing a rich ash to fertilize the ground. Then the

Indians will sometimes wait for a fresh change of season, because the first rain of a new wet season is the most favourable time for planting to begin.

Each family in the yano cultivates its own plot within the gardens, an area of up to two acres forming a typical allotment. One hot day, I went out with one of the yano's older residents to observe the effort required to keep a plot in good condition. I was immediately impressed by the amount of organization evident in his patch. Fine stands of plantains stood next to groves of manioc, while above them rose tall peach palms and a few scattered papaya trees. Closer inspection revealed other, smaller groupings of plants; there were stands of sugar-cane, maize, taro, yams, cane for making arrows, cotton plants, tobacco and spiky growths whose fibres were used for rope-making. In addition, other isolated plants, whose uses were mostly magical, were dotted about among the vegetation. The bulbs of certain species, I was told, are ground up and then either set between arrowheads and their shafts or else mixed with *urucu* and rubbed on to the forehead of a hunter or on his dogs to ensure good fortune in the hunt. Others could be powdered and used to win the favours of a loved one, or cast clandestinely on visitors from other yanos with whom disputes had arisen, to make them ill.

The origins of the Yanomami's plants remain a matter of controversy. Some of the staples, such as manioc and peach palm, appear to be indigenous, while others, including bananas, were perhaps introduced after the Spanish conquest. Some hybridization must have taken place in the unremembered past, for certain of the indigenous plants, including maize as well as peach palm, do not grow in the wild.

The old man I had accompanied was as familiar with the various growths in his patch as any Western gardener with the contents of his plot. While his dogs sat nearby, scratching themselves and occasionally barking at the other people working in the garden, he set about some weeding preparatory to planting manioc cuttings. Squatting on his haunches while he worked, he had soon cleared a space a few yards in extent with expert blows of his machete. Then, using a metal hoe, he broke the ground, piling the earth into neat hummocks. Next he took a bundle of previously collected manioc stems, each about two feet long. Cutting each stem in half, he planted six of the shoots in each prepared mound, pushing them deep into the earth so that only a couple of inches of the stem protruded. Once that job was accomplished, he cut several small plantain shoots from around a stump left where a fully grown plant had been cut down; these he trimmed to make them ready for planting elsewhere in his plot.

The Indians seldom spend more than a few hours a day in their gardens, and on many days do no work there at all. Yet the yield from their banana crop exceeds that obtained on most commercial plantations in central America. All this is achieved, moreover, with virtually no damage to the forest environment. Once the thin soil starts to lose its fertility, after two or three years of cultivation, the yano dwellers simply abandon the old allotments and carve a new area for cultivation at the edge of the existing garden.

Eventually, when all the easily available land has been used, a whole new garden will be cleared, equally close to the yano but in some other direction. Even when untended and clogged with scrub, the old garden will continue to bear some crops to supplement the produce of the new one, and the Indians will continue to visit it occasionally to take advantage of this bounty. Otherwise they will leave it for the forest to reclaim. As a result, the land is almost infinitely re-usable. The soil is able to regenerate completely, and no irreversible imbalance is created in the natural habitat, while its produce, together with the wealth of other foods available from the surrounding forest, provides the Indians with a satisfying and varied diet. Certainly the community at Toototobi struck me as being healthy and well nourished.

I found it easy enough to understand and appreciate the material aspects of life in the yano and the adjoining garden, but Yanomami social relations proved tougher terrain. To begin with, there was the problem of finding out individuals' names. It was no problem to discover the Christian names given to everyone at Toototobi by the missionaries, but the Indians themselves rarely used these foreign appellations. Their own Yanomami names were much harder to elicit because it is considered extremely disrespectful to use a man's name within his hearing. The Yanomami word for "to insult" is the same term used to describe calling someone by his name in public, and to do

so is a serious offence that can sometimes lead to retaliation by sorcery or physical violence. As a result, individuals must be referred to by an elaborate series of cross-references.

The only exceptions to this rule are children up to the age of puberty, because such youngsters are not full actors in the social scene. So adults are often identified by their relationships with the young, for instance as "the father of A", "the brother of B" or, if promised in marriage to a junior, "the husband of C". All three may, of course, be the same person.

More complicated verbal gymnastics are performed when strangers visit the yano. On one such occasion I heard a host ask a child to deliver a message to someone he described as the "the guest I addressed as 'father-in-law', who hung his hammock by the hearth of my father". When this proved insufficient to enlighten the child, the man went on: "He is not very big, and there is a knife hanging by the side of his hammock; yesterday my daughter gave him plantain soup." It took five cross-checking clues to identify one man!

One side-effect of these elaborate circumlocutions is to teach youngsters the network of family relationships within the yano. Such information is vital, for it is inconceivable for a Yanomami to have any form of contact with another individual unless there is some kinship connection between them. Even within the confined world of a yano, however, it is unusual for an indi-

**Sitting among the stores of fruit kept on a shelf above her family's hearth, a little girl succumbs to the temptation of a bunch of ripe bananas. Her arms and legs are smeared with purple palm-fruit juice—a popular drink of the Yanomami—and urucu dye.**

vidual to be directly related by blood or marriage to every other member of the community. So the Indians extend the application of kinship terms beyond their real kin to include people to whom they are not directly related. In other words, one man may choose to call another man "son" or "brother-in-law", even though there is no real link between them. By so doing, he extends to that man much of the good will that would otherwise be reserved only for real family members.

Usually the terms of reference for such extensions of family ties are deduced from the relationships already established by the individual's parents. When such a basis does not exist—for example, in the rare eventuality of contacting new groups—the Indians bestow kinship titles on the basis of personal sympathy or potential advantage. The objective is to form alliances, which can then be consolidated through marriage or the exchange of goods. Such extended relationships aim to ensure solidarity and social continuity, and by and large the system works extraordinarily well.

Each of the different forms of kinship implies important obligations and commitments. A special relationship, for example, exists between a man and his father-in-law, who alone has the right to give an adult Yanomami orders, and to whom total loyalty and respect are due. For marriage often severs the ties binding a man to his own male kin, and particularly to his brothers, who may represent competition for the attentions of his wife. By contrast, a husband will remain on friendly terms with his mother and sisters.

One of the principal motivating forces for young Yanomami males is the desire to impress prospective fathers-in-law, for there is a surplus of males in the Yanomami population that can sometimes cause fierce competition for the favours of girls of marriageable age. At Toototobi, for example, there was a good-looking youth called Helio who tried constantly to behave as a model son-in-law should. He was already married to a widow older than himself; but the Yanomami are not always monogamous, and the widow's father had promised him her much younger sister if he faithfully served the family until the younger girl reached puberty. Although he had once had a reputation as a Lothario, he had now mended his ways and strove at all times to appear hard-working and conscientious, acting in a manner of which any man with a daughter could be expected to approve. His reformed behaviour had not, however, interfered with his innate vanity and sartorial elegance. He was always one of the best painted and decorated individuals in the yano, with fresh feathers through his ears and lower lip, and there still seemed to be an ill-concealed glint of mischief in his eyes.

Even if a man succeeds in currying favour with a father-in-law, he will always continue to treat him with a respectful restraint. When dealing with a mother-in-law, such restraint blossoms into real awe. Like her counterparts round the world, a Yanomami mother-in-law reserves the right to criticize her daughter's husband with a bluntness that no one else would dare to use in his hearing. Such verbal assaults are generally made in a loud voice to the community at large and the son-in-law can do nothing to retaliate. As a result, he is likely to avoid her company at all times. When that is not possible,

Their cotton aprons and strings of beads lie
abandoned on the bank as a group of women
and children enjoy their daily dip in the
river. Above their heads, sunlight catches on
the pale wings of a flight of butterflies.

he may hide from her gaze behind a screen of leaves. Merely catching her eye, the Yanomami say, "makes the heart pound".

True friends and partners for trading, working and hunting are chosen from among a man's brothers-in-law. These may either be the real thing—husbands of his sisters or brothers of his wife—in which case he will co-operate with them closely; or they may be others to whom the title has been extended, in which case a less intense relationship of joking camaraderie will apply. Men so related frequently and demonstratively express affection for each other. Often they will embrace like long-lost friends, even though they may live at adjoining hearths of the same yano.

Bruce had already acquired several such brothers-in-law during the time he had spent with the Indians at Catrimani. Two of these had subsequently moved to Toototobi, one being our host Mateus, and through them the network was rapidly extended. Victor and I were considered to be Bruce's "brothers", and so were comfortingly included under the same title.

The brother-in-law relationship is crucial for a man not only for itself, but also because the Yanomami concept of incest forbids men to have sexual relationships with mothers, sisters, daughters, mothers-in-law, daughters-in-law and nieces, whether real or classified as such. In practice, almost every woman a man knows will fall into one of these prohibited categories, except for the sisters of his real or imagined brothers-in-law, who will thus be the only women with whom marriage is possible.

In the relatively infrequent case of a man having two or more wives, each wife will maintain a hearth of her own, and the husband will live with the current favourite. Girls generally marry soon after puberty, but men rather older—typically in their twenties—for they normally have to earn the right to marry by working for their future parents-in-law for several years. Such bride service, which involves the provision of meat and other foodstuffs and labour in the gardens, demonstrates the groom's capability as a provider.

The relationship between husband and wife is based on a strict definition of each partner's role. The men hunt, build the yano, work in the gardens and protect the community. The women collect firewood and garden produce, prepare food and look after the small children. For much of the day, when the men are out in the garden or the forest, the women dominate the yano.

At Toototobi, both sexes appeared to accept their complementary roles contentedly, and relations between them were generally good. Yet areas of friction existed as in any other society, and often the cause was jealousy. I saw a striking example of this phenomenon during my stay. It involved the most beautiful woman in the yano, a 20-year-old called Celina. She was quietly making manioc bread one day when some of the older women came to tell her that her husband, Rehi, had been seen attempting to seduce another girl down by the river.

When Rehi returned to the yano, his infuriated wife confronted him with her knowledge. Rehi in his turn lost his temper and struck her a glancing blow with his machete which, by ill fortune, happened to be in his hand. The blade was partly deflected by Celina's beads, which scattered on the ground. Nevertheless, she received a cut about an inch long on one shoulder.

At once, all hell broke loose. Most of the other women took Celina's side in the dispute, yelling accusations at Rehi. The din started babies howling and dogs barking. Celina, in her fury, grabbed a large stave. Weeping, she stood over Rehi with the pole clasped in both hands, while her supporters urged her to hit him. Rehi's anger had subsided, and he sat impassively in his hammock, looking the other way as though unaware of his wife.

Usually in such situations a woman can expect to be defended by her relatives, but Celina had been born in another yano and had no immediate male kin at Toototobi. Now, however, support came from an unexpected quarter. Mateus, egged on by his wife, shouted, "I call her sister and will defend her. If I had a club, I would hit the brute myself." At that, he sat down and began to whittle a club from palmwood, all the while muttering angrily to himself.

Celina could not bring herself to hit her husband, however, and before Mateus had finished the weapon, the tension had died down. When we went to see how serious Celina's wound was, we found her more concerned with picking up her broken string of beads than with her injury, which was slight, though bloody. One of the village elders had watched the fracas distractedly from his hammock near us. His only comment was to say: "It's all wrong. A man shouldn't hit his wife with a machete. He should use a stick!"

Such violence was atypical of the generally peaceful and harmonious family life of the yano and the ordered pattern of relationships that underlay it. In the interlocking nexus of family ties, the allegiance of relatives is the key to status and influence in the community, and the man with the widest web of real kinsmen usually assumes the role of headman. Few peoples have less of a social hierarchy than the Yanomami, and the headman's position is correspondingly titular rather than coercive. Nonetheless, the position carries some prestige. Visitors from distant communities, for example, are never addressed by other members of the community in any but the most casual way until they have spent some time talking to the headman.

Such authority as the headman is able to exercise is consultative and advisory only. He is expected regularly to address the yano at large with a mixture of suggestions and recommendations known as *hereamu*, or Headman Talk. The usual time for such discourses is very early in the morning, as much as an hour before first light. The headman's message is, therefore, fed into the first, dawning consciousness of the yano dwellers, at a time when they would in any case be considering what to do during the coming day.

Headman Talk is delivered in one version of the formalized language used by the Yanomami for all public pronouncements. In any society without writing or other means of disseminating mass information, it is clearly desirable to have a formal system for the delivery of public communications. In that sense, the special diction used for Headman Talk resembles, for example, the stylized utterances of the town-criers of medieval Europe.

Literally, the word *hereamu* means "to breathe out"—a fitting description, as the manner of speech adopted for it is built on a series of exhalations.

## Making the Daily Bread

A form of unleavened bread made from sweet manioc, a starchy vegetable, is a staple of the Yanomami diet. Normally eaten with meat or oily palm fruits, it can also provide a filling snack by itself. Supplies soon dwindle, and most Yanomami women bake a fresh batch for their families at least once a week.

The time-consuming job stretches over two days. First, a woman must dig up the manioc tubers from her garden plot; about a dozen are needed to make a week's supply of bread for a family of three. After carrying the tubers home to her hearth, she peels and washes them,

then grates them on a scraper made by punching holes through a flattened tin can. Before they had access to cans, the Yanomami used to grate manioc on flat stones or the bark of a forest tree.

After grating, the woman puts the pulp in a flexible basket, and squeezes it to extract the juice. She then leaves the dough to dry out. The following day, she crumbles and sieves the dough into flour, which is spread out on a large clay plate over her hearth. After baking for about five minutes, the flat loaves are left to cool, then stacked away in a basket or piled on a shelf until they are needed.

**A woman grates manioc tubers into dough in a wooden trough (above). Next day, she sieves the dough and spreads it on a clay plate for baking over her fire (right). Cooked loaves are left to cool on a nearby log.**

58

Forced breathing produces a succession of phrases, each one concluding abruptly on a rhyming vowel sound. Other formalized speech patterns with differing rhythms and techniques are used for other public utterances, when visiting Yanomami come to the yano to invite the inhabitants to a feast, or, during such feasts, to exchange news or engage in trade and barter.

The headman at Toototobi was a small, wiry man whose Christian name was Antonio. He sported a sergeant's military moustache, an apparently permanent tobacco quid, and a pot belly. He was away when we first arrived, and my initial meeting with him was inauspicious. I had been lying in my hammock with my notebook trying to work, although constantly distracted by horseflies and small children. I looked up to find an unprepossessing man with cold, rheumy eyes extending a hand in greeting. I clasped the proffered hand amiably enough, but with my left hand, which happened to be the nearest to the newcomer. Antonio angrily threw this down and insisted on shaking hands properly with the right hand. Thereafter I detected a certain coldness in his attitude towards me.

It was an unfortunate lapse on my part, for like all headmen Antonio was well connected. He owed his position chiefly to the fact that he had three adult married daughters and two others promised in marriage, as well as a married sister. His female relations thereby provided him with six adult male in-laws, all of whom owed their primary allegiance to him. In addition, he had three young, unmarried sons. None of the other men in the yano could boast a comparable network of alliances.

Antonio's Headman Talk was usually concerned with practical matters, such as jobs that needed urgent attention. He might announce that it was time to start planting bananas or that he had heard from a hunter that fruit was ripening somewhere in the forest. If tracks of game had been seen nearby, he would announce it; and he might suggest a fishing trip to a certain pond at a timely moment before the rains began. He offered no more than suggestions; each family was free to take its own decision.

Although Antonio reserved the prerogative of initiating collective decisions and of defining the community's attitudes towards outsiders, there were other people at Toototobi who would occasionally address the yano at large. In general, they were the elders of the community, who also had the right to interrupt Antonio's discourse in public if they disagreed with him; no one else would go further than to mutter dissent to his neighbour. Chief among the old men were Severiano and Tiago, who tended to concentrate their public pronouncements on matters of history, myth and ritual. Sometimes they would explain the form that a forthcoming ceremony should take, or would recount one of the innumerable Yanomami myths to anyone who cared to listen; on other occasions they merely recalled dreams they had had during the night, or stories of events that had befallen the group in the past.

During the day, when the younger men were out hunting, the yano was occupied by the women, a few elderly men such as Severiano and Tiago, and the children. Although the women tended to regard the yano at such times as

A youngster gnaws contentedly on a stick of sugar-cane while he watches one of his neighbours preparing to return to the yano from her garden. A bark sling attached to the basket is looped over her head to support her load—some 50 pounds of plantains.

their domain, there was no question as to which of the three groups was most immediately and inescapably noticeable. The play packs of children of both sexes, roaming the central plaza in search of amusement and shrieking boisterously at one another as they did so, dominated the building by the sheer exuberance of their energy and invention.

Up to about the age of three, infants have very close contact with their mothers at all times. After they have been weaned, or when the next child arrives—whichever comes earlier—they begin to look after themselves and are allowed a degree of independence shared by few of their counterparts in Western countries. They are even free to take their little hammocks and go to sleep with their grandmothers. Their time is fully occupied playing all day with the other children.

The children's education is a continuous process of observation and practice. There is no formal teaching. Instead, they are left to their own devices to discover, simply by watching and imitating the adults, what it means to be a Yanomami: how to hunt, cook, garden and make things; what to collect from the forest and what to avoid; and above all how to behave in dealing with friends and foes—and with the spirits.

When Yanomami men talk about their past, they divide their youth into three clearly defined stages. First, there is the time of infancy with their mothers; then childhood, from roughly three to 13 years of age, when they are with the play packs, learning to hunt with miniature bows and arrows; and finally, from the age of 14 or 15 onwards, adolescence, leading into adulthood, when they start to hunt in earnest with full-size weapons.

A notable feature of this pattern of childhood is the sandwich effect: the boys are closely tied to adults in infancy and adolescence, but in between they enjoy a long, independent period with their own kind. During that time, they spend relatively little time at the hearths of their own families, only going there to eat and sleep. Instead, they learn from a wide spectrum of other adults, whose hearths they visit.

At Toototobi, the boys in the play packs were tirelessly cheeky and energetic. They were seldom without their miniature bows and arrows, from which no small creature was safe. One of their leaders was Donaldo, a 10-year-old who loved to climb the trees outside the yano. He could often be seen standing in the topmost branches, casually abandoning his handhold to throw down edible fruits. To describe his climbing skill, the villagers said he had "sticky hands"—an expression also used of monkeys.

Girls, too, are to be found in the play packs, though they tend to spend more time than boys in the company of adults. At Toototobi, the girls often gave the impression of being everywhere at the same time. At one moment a 10-year-old might be working with the older women, helping with babies, fetching water or going on collecting expeditions into the forest. The next moment she might be romping in the plaza with a mixed group of other girls and boys. Typical of this group was Helio's stepdaughter, Lorena. She was one of the most vivacious children imaginable, and was always beautifully painted and decorated. The way she managed to remain neat and enchanting

On a section of the yano roof that still awaits its covering of thatch, a young boy playfully stalks a tame Spix's guan—a bird of the same family as the curassows. As well as dogs, a variety of small animals and birds are kept as pets by the Toototobi community.

during the wildest and most animated games never failed to astonish me.

The girls' range of alternatives only comes to an end as they approach puberty. At the age of roughly 13, they no longer join in communal games, but instead join the adult female world. During adolescence they are closely protected by the older women, for the world is suddenly full of predatory males. At the time of their first menstruation, they are isolated for a few days in a shelter constructed inside the yano, an event that marks the transition from childhood to adulthood. From that time on, they are considered of marriageable age, and normally find a partner soon after.

Watching the children at play one afternoon, I soon found out just how closely their games were related to the roles they would play in adult life. At first, three of the older boys, aged about 10 to 12, pretended to be hunters confronting peccaries, while the girls and smaller boys realistically took the part of their quarry, repeatedly charging them so that they had to climb up building poles to escape. Then the game changed and one of the hunters became a tapir, fighting off an attack by hunters' dogs. Tiring of life as a dog, another boy suddenly became a jaguar; the girls rushed off screaming as he tried to bite them, only to return bravely to the attack when the smallest of their number was caught. The play became rough, though still good-humoured. Shrieking happily, the girls removed their aprons and lost their decorations. Finally the game ended in tears, when one of the smallest children was accidentally hurt and retired screaming to his family.

When the group reassembled half an hour later, the mood was more subdued. At an empty hearth they had appropriated for their own uses, they had established a complete replica of an adult home, with its own small fire and miniature hammocks slung in two tiers between building poles. The children built a toy smoking-platform and set it over the fire. They then set about grilling four lizards and a small snake, which had been killed earlier in the day. This was play food, not fit to be eaten, but the youngsters devoted quite as much care and attention to its preparation as their elders would have shown in readying a real meal. In addition to cooking the meat in a little tin, they performed all the other chores attendant on mealtime, using three minute gourds to fetch water and a couple of small baskets to carry fruit.

The secure and happy image the children presented as they concentrated on their tasks struck me all the more forcibly because of the wide publicity that has in the past been given to one of the Yanomami's less attractive practices, infanticide. Unwanted children are often killed at birth. The motives for such a decision vary. A woman may, for instance, dispose of her baby if it seems deformed or sickly, if she herself is ill or otherwise unfit to raise her offspring, or if there is no father to feed the child. One of a pair of twins is usually killed, because the intensity of the care that Yanomami mothers devote to their children in the first three years of their lives makes it impractical to handle two at a time. For the same reason, a new baby that comes when a mother is still suckling her previous child may be dispatched to prevent the elder child from becoming *totishi*—an almost untranslatable word best rendered as "deprived". A boy or girl child may also be killed if he or she arrives

In the warm light of the setting sun, a family
enjoys a relaxed evening meal of meat and
boiled plantain. They use small wooden
sticks to spear each mouthful of food from a
cooking pot that rests at one side of the
fire, within easy reach of the hammocks.

after three or four previous children of the same sex, as a balance of sons and daughters is considered necessary.

In Toototobi, the missionaries had done everything in their power to discourage the practice, and there was some evidence that their efforts were having an effect. The social need for infanticide in keeping the population in balance with the available resources had also diminished, as imported diseases had for the past two decades kept the Yanomami's numbers in check. The results were not always unfailingly positive, however, for, repugnant though it may seem, infanticide fulfilled some social functions. We had evidence of this next door to us in the yano, for Mateus's wife, Sonia, had a child who was *totishi,* being little more than a year older than his younger brother. He was noticeable as the only child in the yano who cried regularly, noisily and at length, and he was clearly unhappy and disturbed.

A Yanomami mother always goes outside the yano to give birth, and no man may follow her. If a woman does decide to dispose of her offspring, she will do it in the forest immediately after the infant is born. The site of the killing is significant, for by killing the baby outside of the yano, the mother indicates that it is not part of the community; once a baby is brought into the yano, there is no risk to its life. The usual method employed to accomplish the deed is to suffocate the child by putting a leaf down its throat. The killing is always done in the absence of men, a fact that gives the women some control over the reproduction rate and sex ratio of the group.

However much one may deplore infanticide, it is certainly unfair to the Yanomami to suggest that its practice implies an inhuman or uncaring attitude towards children. In fact, the Indians treat their offspring with great affection, and their commitment to the welfare of any child accepted into the yano is total. Indeed, a yano must be one of the most reassuring environments in which a child can grow up. Instead of having only a nuclear family surrounded by strangers, the children are kin to, or have a close relationship with, everyone they know, so they need never feel isolated or rejected.

Such thoughts on the security of Yanomami childhood came to me one afternoon when, finding it too hot to work, I took a book and went down to the river to read and swim. I bathed with the boys' play pack, who attacked and splashed me until I said "Enough", at which point they politely left me to sit on the rocks by a small rapid and contemplate the scene. The river hurried past over the black rocks, beige and faster-flowing than when we had first arrived, as a result of some early rain up in the hills. A pair of green-and-red kingfishers darted upstream like messengers on an urgent mission, and a large horsefly with bright green eyes reminded me that I was in the heart of the tropics. Soon after, the women came down to bathe with the rest of the children. As the two groups splashed happily together in the dark water, they struck me as an enduring image of the spontaneous affection that underlines the Yanomami's relationship with the young.

That evening I experienced a deeper, almost mystical insight into the sense of well-being and protection that the yano itself can offer. Perhaps my brain

Two vine baskets, dyed with the red juice of the urucu plant, hang outside their owner's home to show he is willing to trade them, perhaps for a new hammock or a bow. The red colouring distinguishes the baskets as the work of a neighbouring group of Yanomami who occasionally visit Toototobi and barter for knives and machetes.

was more than usually impressionable, for earlier we had been brought a leaf package of large white mushrooms that had been gathered by the women on their way back from the gardens. They had a good, strong taste and a pleasantly chewy texture. The thought crossed my mind that they might be hallucinogenic, but I had no way of finding out for sure.

The moon was full that night, poised like a weak sun in a hazy sky, with a clear halo ringing it. The world was flooded with a pale light that was bright enough to read by. Before going to sleep, I left the yano to go for a walk through the forest. Tropical nights can be magical, soft and friendly. The sound of the frogs and cicadas was muted, and the outlines of trees seemed etched on an opaque background like scenes from a Chinese watercolour. Mist lay in the hollows. In a state of near-euphoria, I wandered barefoot along a narrow track, torchless and unconcerned about snakes or biting fire-ants. Convinced that all evil was absent, I felt that no predator would interfere with me on such a night, when the moon in full strength was watching over me. I felt sorry for anyone not sharing this moment with me, even for the Yanomami, who rarely go out at night for fear of snakes and spirits.

Returning, I walked the last familiar stretch, past the clearing where the Yanomami had had their previous dwelling and where a few remaining charred poles pointed blackened fingers at the sky. As I emerged from the brake of forest that cloaked my destination, I stopped, surprised. The yano had vanished. Straining my eyes and staring straight at where I knew it to be, I saw only misty space between the trees, grey, insubstantial and empty.

Were the mushrooms I had eaten really hallucinogenic? Was I dreaming? As I stepped closer, the faintest outline of a gentle curve began to appear through the haze, but so well camouflaged against the forest background that it was not until I was almost at the entrance that I could see the whole familiar shape of the building, set down like a flying saucer from another planet on a bed of mist, on which it seemed to float. Parting the loose palm fronds that masked the low doorway, I passed from one world to another. Inside, everything was familiar and secure; the Indians lay sleeping in their hammocks, warmed by the fires. Overwhelmed by feelings of tenderness and fellowship, I made my way to my appointed hearth and climbed into my hammock, where for hours I lay sleepless, listening to the crickets that sang softly above each hearth all through the night.

66

## Private Moments in a Public Place

Few people live their lives more publicly than the Yanomami. The yanos they inhabit are homes to whole communities, often numbering 100 people or more. Yet within each structure's thatched wall, every family has its own separate hearth, where its members eat, sleep and store their belongings. The hearths provide areas of privacy where individuals can go about their business undisturbed in the deep shade of the building's roof.

For much of the day the yano is left to the women, children and old people, while the men go out to work in the gardens or to hunt in the forest. At such times the building offers the tranquil spectacle of mothers playing

Surrounded by dense forest, a yano near the Toototobi river lies open to the sun. About 20 families live at adjoining hearths around the building's

with their babies, sweeping the floor around the hearths, weaving baskets or aprons, or simply relaxing in hammocks near their fires. Meanwhile packs of older children wander through the dwelling, improvising games. When the hunters return to the yano in the afternoon, the pace of life quickens: families visit other hearths to share out the day's catch or simply to circulate the latest gossip, and food is cooked for the evening meal. Sunset finds the Indians preparing for the coming night. But conversations continue to resound across the plaza for an hour or two after dark, until the last voices die away and the community settles down to sleep.

roofed perimeter. The central plaza is communal space and everyone co-operates to keep it clean, especially when visitors are expected for a feast.

68

Relaxing in a cotton hammock, a young wife with her baby in her lap strings china beads from a gourd bowl on to a thread to make a necklace. Above her an older child, already weaned, lies daydreaming in a similar berth.

While his son peeks through the parted strands, a father concentrates on finishing a hammock that his wife has been weaving round a wooden frame at the family hearth. To make the bedding, a single length of cotton is wound in continuous strands round the outer posts to form a solid rectangle about five feet long by three feet wide; then additional strands of cotton are woven crosswise and tied with rows of knots.

Using her big toe to stretch a new apron out to its full length, a woman checks that the threads making up the fringe hang evenly. Such aprons, which are dyed red with urucu before use, are worn by all Yanomami females from the age of five or six onwards.

Her torso adorned with strings of beads, a young woman relaxes by her hearth, where an armadillo is curing in its shell over the fire. Smoking helps

to preserve the meat, which will be boiled and eaten after two or three days. In the background, a tame trumpeter bird passes by in search of food.

Playing a hunting game, some young children pretend to be jaguars while others, acting as quarry, take refuge up the yano poles. The climbers have tied their feet together with liana (right) for extra grip on the wood.

76

In the hours of darkness, the yano's perimeter is dotted with flames where, at each hearth (inset), fires burn to warm the sleepers through the night.

# Three | Living Off the Forest's Riches

From the circular clearing surrounding the yano, a network of trails led outwards through the trees like the spokes of a wheel. Besides the well-worn paths to the gardens and the river, used daily by many of the yano-dwellers, a multitude of smaller tracks veined the territory around the building. Some went to the nearest neighbouring yanos, several hours' or days' walk away from Toototobi, and so outside the normal daily orbit of our hosts. Others led deep into the uninhabited forest.

The less-used trails, which mostly branched off the tracks that led to the gardens, followed almost invisible routes through the forest, marked only by such signs as an occasional stretch of trodden earth, a patch of scraped bark or a tree stump notched with a machete blow. Like all forest peoples, the Yanomami regularly break and bend over the stems of plants and branches as they walk along, to indicate the way for fellow-hunters and to guide themselves safely on their return. When crossing country off the trail, a hunter will do this every few yards, and to his trained eye the reversed leaves and cut stems stand out as clear signals marking his route.

The trails traversed a monochrome world, permanently shaded by the high canopy of the leaves. At ground level, bright colours were remarkable by their rarity. Among the few common flowering plants I noticed were a yellow-flowered relation of the familiar "red-hot poker"; a small bush whose branches were festooned with clusters of delicate, white, candelabra-shaped blossoms; and a member of the *Cephaelis* family whose small yellow blooms cradled in red leaves resemble snapdragons in shape, if not in colour. Elsewhere toadstools of red, yellow and white provided spots of brightness on the huge, spreading roots of the larger trees, and butterflies of shiny enamel-blue drifted languidly past; but the general effect was of an endless variety of greens and browns in an apparently uninhabited world. Only when I stopped to sit on a felled branch or lean against a tree trunk and listen to the

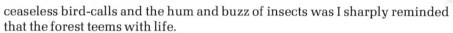

ceaseless bird-calls and the hum and buzz of insects was I sharply reminded that the forest teems with life.

Indeed, more than two-thirds of the world's estimated four and a half million species of plants and animals live in tropical forests. Only a small fraction have so far been named and catalogued. The forest is the richest, least explored environment on earth, and nowhere is its life more varied than in the Amazon basin, the world's largest tract of continuous tree cover.

Over the past 100 million years, the Amazon rain forest has served as a forcing-house for the evolution of species, with multiple varieties of each one developing to fill every possible nook and cranny of the ecosystem. The result has been an extreme diversification; the forest has no fewer than 319 varieties of hummingbirds, and the plant life is correspondingly varied. Nor are there anywhere clusters of a single predominant species; all specimens of a single plant are usually scattered at wide intervals through the forest rather than gathered in stands, as in European woods.

The Yanomami are familiar with this complex world, and exploit the forest's diversity by hunting its larger animals and gathering smaller creatures and useful plants. An astounding range of plant and animal life is collected in this manner. Some 200 plants are put to use, providing food, medicines, hallucinogenic drugs, poisons for fishing, building materials, gums, dyes, containers, cords and other essentials of Indian life. Many kinds of insects, shellfish and small reptiles are also regularly collected, for the Yanomami augment their diet with exotic forest fare such as termites, caterpillars, spiders, frogs and crayfish.

Both hunting and gathering are constant activities for the Indians, but their relative importance—in terms of the food they produce—varies with the time of year. There are no fluctuations between periods of warmth and cold in the rain forest, for in the hours of daylight the heat is constant and humid all year round. The temperature at Toototobi hovers constantly in the 70s and 80s during the daytime, only changing noticeably after sunset, when it drops to 60°F or less. Therefore the seasons are signalled not by alterations in the temperature but by rainfall.

The wet season starts in April, when the first rivers begin to swell as a result of rainfall up in the hills, and reaches its height in June—by which time the Toototobi river has changed from a lethargic stream to a wide and fast-flowing torrent. The season passes as the rainfall gradually diminishes. By October it is back to its April level, and by January and February a week or more may go by with no rain at all. The level of the rivers drops so dramatically that many dry up almost completely.

In terms of the foodstuffs available, each season has its own advantages and disadvantages. During the dry season, hunting conditions are at their best and long journeys can be made through the forest. However, much of the game is scrawny because little fruit, their main food, is available. There are few comestibles to gather in the forest, but plantains and peach palm are ripe in the gardens and the conditions are good for fishing. During the wet season, by contrast, hunting is difficult because the rivers are high and the forest tracks often under water; the rain also tends to hinder tracking by washing away traces of the quarry. In compensation, however, any prey that the hunters do succeed in killing is likely to be in good condition, because wild fruits are abundant. At the height of the wet season, in June and July, when hunting is at its worst and the gardens are producing little, gathering provides the main daily sustenance.

Even at less propitious times of year, gathering the natural produce of the forest is a constant, vital daily activity. It is principally a job for the women, who go out in small groups, often accompanied by young girls who help with the collecting or look after their older companions' babies. By contrast, the men rarely make special trips to gather anything other than honey or palm fruits. While out hunting, however, they will keep an eye open for any collectable food resources, and either bring them back themselves or else pass on information about them to the women.

Occasionally, however, gathering takes on a more communal air. A camp site of temporary shelters may be constructed in the forest, so that a group of people can spend a few days collecting and hunting. I took part in one such venture in the course of an overnight excursion to gather peach-palm fruit from a site six hours' walk away from Toototobi. The trip was in itself hardly typical of gathering expeditions, for the fruit was not wild, but instead grew in an abandoned garden, near a yano the people of Toototobi had left almost 20 years before our visit, when they moved to their present home. But the atmosphere was similar, and in the course of the 15-mile journey along almost invisible paths, I got an insight into the way in which the Yanomami make the most of their forest environment.

The trip was arranged at the suggestion of Antonio; he had heard from a visitor who had recently passed that way that the peach-palm fruit was

The soft, fleshy fruits of the peach-palm tree (above) are a delicacy to the Yanomami. But it takes ingenuity and daring to reach the ripe clusters, which grow some 40 feet up trunks bristling with razor-sharp barbs. One method of climbing the tree (right) is to use twin sets of poles lashed together crosswise, so that they clamp on to the trunk. The climber rests his weight on one set while lifting the other; by arching his body and raising his hands and his feet alternately, he moves like a caterpillar up to his goal.

ripening. Within minutes of announcing the news during his morning Headman Talk, the few essentials for an overnight camp—hammocks, cooking pots, and a bunch or two of plantains to provide food for the journey—had been thrown into empty baskets and people were already leaving.

The party, consisting of most of the inhabitants of the yano, spread out over a mile or more along a faint trail that led northwards through the forest. The young men led the procession, partly in the hope of surprising and killing game *en route*, partly to clear the path. The women stayed together in a group at the rear. I travelled with the older men, somewhere in the middle.

A sense of excitement and fun ran throughout the line of people. The Yanomami love these expeditions and, at times when game is scarce near the yano and the gardens are unproductive, will sometimes set off *en masse* to camp in the forest simply because they feel like a holiday. About once every 90 minutes, the column would halt for a rest. During these pauses the men would examine their arrows, checking the shafts for straightness, bending them back into shape if they seemed warped, and occasionally honing the tips. Then the hunters would set off again, the rest of the column taking their places behind them. As we moved forward, there was a constant murmur of conversation as individuals noted squirrels and birds in the trees, animal tracks on the ground, or fruit beginning to ripen.

We reached the vicinity of the old garden early in the afternoon, and the menfolk at once set about erecting open-sided overnight shelters for their families. The roofing in each case was made from wild banana leaves gathered in the surrounding forest; the thatch was supported by horizontal crosspieces of palm wood lashed on to a triangular wooden frame resting on three poles, between five and seven feet high, pushed into the soft ground. In little more time than it took me to hang up my hammock, the frames of half a dozen of these simple lean-tos were up.

After barely a moment's rest we were all on our feet again, ready to make our way to the gardens in search of peach palms. The visitor's report had not been wrong. Great clusters of red, orange, yellow and green fruit adorned the trees, which rose in clumps from land that, after lying fallow for so long, had become almost indistinguishable from the surrounding forest. At first sight, however, they seemed unreachable, for the fruit grows just below the crowns, about 50 feet above the ground, and the trees have sharp, black spines all the way up their trunks.

The Yanomami, though, have their ways. One is to loop a length of liana around the palm, then, while holding both ends of the loop, to climb some neighbouring, smooth-trunked tree. To gain purchase, the climber ties his feet together with a small piece of liana; by gripping the trunk between his insteps, he can secure a firm enough foothold to raise himself upwards. On reaching treetop level, he pulls the palm tree's crown towards him by means of the liana, and prises off the heavy bunches of fruit, which are then tied to another liana and lowered to the ground.

When there is no smooth tree within reach of the peach palm, a fruit-gatherer will use an ingenious method of climbing the palm itself without

Searching for titbits to add to her cooking pot, a woman reaches into the subterranean burrow of a land crab and feels gingerly for its occupant. If she finds the crab, she will kill it as quickly as possible to avoid injury from its menacing claws, and will then add it to the rest of the day's haul in the leaf pouch that she holds in her left hand.

touching the spines. This involves some quite sophisticated engineering, using two pairs of poles. Each pair is arranged in an X-shape, then lashed together at the joint with liana. The two crosses are then set against the base of the tree to be climbed and each loosely tied around its trunk with another length of liana. Secured in this fashion, the poles make two platforms that the climber can raise, the upper with his hands, the lower with his feet, up the trunk of the tree. When pressure is exerted on them, they wedge tight and do not slip. Climbing the palm is nonetheless hard work, as it involves arching and straightening the body repeatedly just inches away from the protruding spines. Having reached the top, the climber strips the tree of bunches of fruit, which he lowers to the ground with a length of liana. He may then use a long pole—passed up to him attached to the same cord—to remove the fruit from the tops of other trees within reach. Sometimes whole bunches fall accidentally during this operation, and then they explode like grenades, scattering the fruit across the forest floor.

After harvesting the fruit, the Yanomami returned to camp carrying huge loads and set about preparing a meal. The fruit had to be boiled to make it edible; it tasted tart and fibrous, and had a stone in the middle that was discarded. Pulped into a juice, it is very popular for feasts, and indeed that day's crop was consumed at such a gathering two days later.

In the shelters that night, everyone seemed to be laughing or telling stories, and the atmosphere was as frivolous as at a school dormitory party. There was excitement when a cayman was spotted in the river. The young men at once went off to hunt it, and succeeded in killing it with a stick sharpened to serve as a spear. The meat was shared out and grilled. I ate some that night, and I swear that for taste and texture it rivalled any lobster or crayfish tail I have eaten in the best restaurants of Europe.

During the evening the women made an excursion into the surrounding forest. Each took a brand from the fire burning in her hearth and waved it up and down like a sparkler at a Christmas festival to light her way. They returned at speed, weaving in groups through the undergrowth and convulsed with laughter. One of them, it turned out, thought that she had seen a snake and her momentary panic had set them giggling. The incident was funny enough to keep people chortling all around the camp for the rest of the evening. Fresh incidents revived the hilarity, which reached a peak when a cord supporting the hammock of one of the young bachelors suddenly broke, tipping him into his fire beneath.

In spite of the hard day of walking and fruit-gathering behind them, everyone seemed wide awake and full of fun. It was only in the dark watches of the night that a deep silence finally fell, interrupted by the occasional shriek of an animal or bird, the cry of children in their sleep, and sometimes the low murmuring of a sleepless couple.

Long before dawn, the level of conversation began to rise again. By the time the first pale shadows began to show, there was animated talk all around as the Indians cheerfully discussed the day's plans. The women sat in their hammocks, playing with their babies or picking lice from each other's hair. Every now and then someone would explode into giggles, recalling some incident of the previous night.

By first light, everyone was up, preparing to return to the yano. The vast quantities of peach palm awaiting transportation were gathered into heaps, stripped of their stems, and packed in carrying baskets or back-packs made of interwoven palm fronds, supported by a bark strap worn around the carrier's forehead. Using the dye from *urucu* pods found growing in the old garden, some of the women applied a light coat of body make-up. Then, when everyone was ready, we set off homewards. We walked fast for most of the way, once again stopping for rests every hour or two.

During these pauses, the Indians were always on the look-out for forest resources to exploit. On one halt, Mateus located an *amahi* tree, whose bark provides a component of the Yanomami's hallucinogenic drugs. Within three minutes he had stripped the entire tree, peeling off the bark in thin strips and chopping it into short lengths that he added to his pack. Another man shinned up a twisted liana to a height of about 80 feet to collect some useful lengths of vine. A third hunter threw a hook and line into a muddy pond beside us. Within minutes he had caught three fish; skewered on sticks, they were grilled over an open fire. Meanwhile, the women too were putting the forest to good use, picking fresh green leaves to make decorations for their arms and ears. Like the men, they were completely at home there, knowing the potential of every plant and animal.

Over the next month, I had many other opportunities to see how the Yanomami take advantage of the forest's abundance. One of the most valued of its resources is honey, a delicacy which the Yanomami eat raw and also serve as a drink, diluted with water. The Indians collect at least 15 different types of honey, subtly varying in flavour from sweet to sharp and each the product of a separate species of bee. Some of these build their nests underground or on tree trunks. Most commonly, though, the nests are found high up inside the hollowed branches of trees.

One of the oldest residents of the yano, Tiago, took us with him one afternoon on a trip to a nest he had spotted inside a hollow branch high in the forest canopy. The tree supporting it turned out to be a real giant. With a trunk at least 25 feet in circumference and no branches for the first 60 feet of its height, it looked completely unclimbable.

Tiago, however, managed to shin up one of its neighbours to a height of perhaps 75 feet. From there he swung himself across on to one of the lower branches of the nest-bearing tree. He was still about 50 feet below his goal, and there was nothing but space between him and the branch he was climbing towards. At this point he lowered a liana that he had wrapped around his shoulder, and shouted to us to attach to it two 20-foot poles that he had cut before starting to climb. After pulling up the poles, he positioned one of them on the branch on which he was standing in such a way that the other end rested on the stump of a severed bough protruding from the tree trunk above his head. Having tied its base to the branch with liana, he proceeded to climb

A youngster takes careful aim with his bow and arrow—scaled-down versions of an adult hunter's weapons—at a cricket he and his companion have spotted on the yano floor. On the right, the two boys play at cooking a bag of small reptiles—none of which will be eaten—over a miniature grill.

up the pole. If the loose end had slipped, he would have plunged nearly 100 feet to almost certain death, but he showed no sign of concern.

At this critical juncture, it suddenly began to rain. A roaring downpour rushed across the forest, soaking everything in its path. Tiago only grinned broadly and, by means of the other pole, pulled himself up to the hollow branch holding the bees' nest. Perching near the trunk, he lowered a liana for his axe. It took him half an hour to chop through the limb, during which time the rain continued without a break.

At last the whole branch broke away and fell with a great crash, knocking over the tops and limbs of two fair-sized trees on the way down. Shinning back down to the ground, Tiago was finally able to get at his quarry. Cutting into the branch with his axe, he reached inside and pulled out first the combs in which the young bee grubs live and finally the lower cells, containing about a pound of dark brown honey. Runny and thin, it had a sharp, rather sour taste. Tiago wrapped it in a leaf parcel for taking home. Some combs containing young grubs, we ate on the spot; the Yanomami consider them a delicacy. The flavour of the grubs was strong and quite distinctive; it reminded me of fresh bamboo shoots with a trace of sweet-and-sour sauce.

I found caterpillars rather less to my taste, although they are a regular part of the Yanomami diet. Collected in clusters from the leaves on which they live, the caterpillars are then wrapped neatly in leaf parcels and baked over a fire. One day I saw some green-and-brown specimens being cooked in the yano. In the interests of science and *haute cuisine* I accepted a handful of the shrivelled morsels, which smelled faintly of dried shrimp. The leathery body casing concealed a soft interior that burst into the mouth on chewing. I ate a fair number before deciding that caterpillars do not represent one of nature's hidden culinary delights, and that it would not be a matter for great regret if I never repeated the experience.

Typically for a gathering activity, termite collection was a job for the women, and broken nests from which the contents had been removed were a common sight on the paths near the yano. On one occasion I came upon a party at work on a nest, which they had dislodged from the side of a tree. The big, spherical structure had been cut in half and the two halves perched open-side down on the end of sticks, like umbrellas. One woman tapped each half in turn with a machete. The small, black termites and the much bigger, white grubs fell out on to leaves placed to catch them.

Later, the grubs were roasted in a leaf parcel. The resulting food was neutral in colour, taste and texture, rather like a soggy breakfast cereal. It was, however, extremely rich in nutrients, and it pleased me to think that a few spoonfuls of the pâté provided me with the nutritional equivalent of a pound or more of prime-cut steak. Termites possess weight for weight as much, if not more, protein than beef and nearly three times as many calories.

Other regular additions to the Yanomami diet include frogs and land crabs, both of which are commonly collected by the women. The high season for frogs comes at the start of the rains when the creatures come down from trees or emerge from the undergrowth and gather in small ponds to mate. The characteristic croaking that precedes their congress acts as an alarm bell for the Indians. As soon as they hear it, women in the yano will drop whatever they are doing to follow the sound. They use knives to kill the frogs. After skinning and gutting them, they cook the bodies in leaf parcels. The best time for gathering crabs is slightly later, in May and June. By that time the waters have begun to rise, softening the ground so that the women can dig the crabs out of their burrows at the foot of trees. They stretch their arms into these holes, ignoring the many painful wounds they may receive from the creatures' strong pincers as they pull them out. They then kill their prey by pressing on their nerve centres with their thumbs. The boiled flesh is excellent, the body of the crab being eaten as well as the claws.

Fishing provides valuable food, but takes up little of the Yanomami's time or energy. Only recently and in a few areas have they begun to acquire a knowledge from outside contacts of how to build and use dug-out canoes, and how to fish with hook and line. At Toototobi, even after 20 years of living next to a substantial river, most of the adults were still afraid of water. When bathing, they stayed in the shallows and never went out of their depth, and most disliked wading across the river when the water was high.

There were exceptions to the general aquaphobia. The children and adolescents had grown up close to the river and loved playing in it. One or two of

After opening a termite nest and impaling it on a stick, a woman sorts through insects dislodged from it on to leaves (below). Discarding fully grown adults, she keeps the white grubs (right) to be roasted and eaten.

the men were skilful at shooting fish with their bows and arrows when the river was low, and one hunter even had his own canoe, which he put at the general disposal of the yano.

The most common method of catching fish, however, was for men and women to poison the water of a shallow forest pond. Sometimes the poison was made from the little heart-shaped leaves of a small forest tree that was also cultivated in the gardens; on other occasions it was distilled from the leaves, buds and stems of the spade-shaped *clybadium sylvestre* plant, from the bark of a forest tree, or from certain types of vine. In each case the plants were pounded to a pulp, which was then usually placed in a sieve-like basket; the vines and bark were crushed, then simply tied in a bundle.

I watched Mateus and another man use such a bundle to catch fish in a lagoon surrounded by thick vegetation not far from the yano. They swung the vines in and out of the water, all the while chanting a spell to make the poison powerful. Its juices diffused through the pond, paralyzing the fish's gills so that oxygen could not be absorbed. They were far from dead at that stage, however, and catching them required some skill. The two sexes used different methods to dispatch their prey. The women scooped them out of the water with shallow baskets, sometimes hitting them first with machetes or knives. The men used only arrows, held like spears, to stab their quarry. The accuracy of their aim was exceptional; I saw several tiny fish impaled on arrowheads larger than themselves.

As soon as the fish were dead, the women cleaned and scaled them, and wrapped them in leaves. Later they were grilled in these same leaf parcels over fires back in the yano.

However much the Yanomami welcome the fish, the honey and the other fruits of the forest, gathering lacks the special prestige attached to hunting. For a man, hunting is the overriding topic of interest and the activity upon which his self-esteem and the sense of his own manhood most depend. Even when resting in his hammock, his thoughts will as likely as not turn to the chase. He will constantly take down his arrows to straighten and test them, and his conversations with other men will usually revolve around their experiences in the forest or the location of game in the vicinity. Success as a hunter is strongly associated with a man's sex role, and he will be mocked and rejected by women if he consistently fails to kill. A girl he is pursuing may ask him, "Are you hunting me instead of game?"

I could see that the preoccupation with hunting started in early youth. The boys who made up the play packs constantly kept their bows and arrows near them, and as soon as potential prey was spotted one or more of the children would set off in pursuit. This lethal sport often seemed cruel to my European eyes. I was particularly upset one day when the boys proudly brought me the body of a tiny dark-green hummingbird that I had often watched hovering over the hibiscus outside the hut where I went regularly to write. There were occasions, too, when I felt compelled to put out of their misery lizards and toads that the boys had speared, then freed to spear again.

Constructing a shelter for an overnight stay in the forest, a hunter spreads a thatch of wild banana leaves over crossbeams lashed with liana to a triangular framework of poles. Such unwalled structures, which provide protection from rain and supports for the occupants' hammocks, are used by families on lengthy collecting expeditions and by hunters on sorties in search of game.

Yet the stalking and killing of any creature small enough to fall prey to their miniature arrows was a vital part of their education, training them not to fail when, as adults, they would pursue more necessary prey.

Once the Yanomami reach adulthood, most daily hunting is done alone, or in small groups of two or three. At Toototobi, one of the familiar sights of the yano was a young man striding purposefully out to the forest as day dawned, his bow and arrows clasped firmly under his arm like a sergeant-major's baton and a bamboo quiver, supported by a cord around the neck, hanging down his spine. Only when an important feast was being prepared, to which guests from a neighbouring yano would be invited, did a special group hunt take place. In that case, most or all of the able-bodied hunters in the community would join together to do their share.

Almost all of the creatures of the forest are hunted, but the relatively few large mammals of Amazonia are by far the most prized game. Tapirs, hefty animals that can weigh as much as 650 pounds, are valued most highly, followed by deer and two species of peccary or wild pig—the collared and the white-lipped. Other favourite prey include certain of the larger monkeys, armadillos and capybaras, the world's largest rodents, which can grow to a length of four feet and a weight of 160 pounds. Several of the larger birds, such as the curassows and some parrots, are also good to eat, while smaller birds such as toucans and certain types of hawk are killed for their feathers rather than their flesh. Smaller rodents, among them agouti, squirrels and pacas, are also eaten, as are coati and some ant-eaters.

To kill their prey the Indians have only their bows and arrows. The arrows, however, are formidable weapons, some seven or eight feet long. The shafts are made from canes that are light, straight and full of soft white pulp. At the butt end of the shafts are bound two halves of split currasow feathers. The plumes are naturally curved; by positioning them so that the curves face in different directions, a propellor effect is achieved that provides torque to make the arrow rotate in flight.

Four different types of arrowhead are used, depending on the intended prey. A sharpened blade carved from a strip of bamboo is used for hunting tapir, peccaries and deer, as it causes a wound deep enough to disable these large animals. The blood from the wound also makes the animal easier to follow if it runs off. For shooting birds, the hunter will use either a barbed head made from monkey bone, which will remain secured so that the arrow's weight will drag the bird to the ground even if it is not killed on impact, or alternatively a three-pronged head fashioned from a suitably shaped twig; the latter variety is used to stun small birds, hunted for their feathers, without the risk of blood stains. The fourth type of arrowhead, designed for hunting monkeys, is simply a long, thin point of black palm wood, notched so that it will break off and stay in the body of the victim. Such heads are coated with the drug named *yakoana*, which the Yanomami themselves use as a hallucinogen. It also, however, acts as a muscle relaxant, and prevents the monkey from holding on to a branch and so perhaps dying high up on a tree, its muscles still locked in spasm.

The inhabitants of Toototobi did not, like many Yanomami, have access to curare to tip their arrowheads. The vine from which the poison is made grows only at higher altitudes, and the nearest plants were nearly 50 miles away from Toototobi, up the Demini river. One day some of the older men, who were grouped around Antonio's hammock to chat with a visitor from that region, showed me two lethal barbs he had brought with him for purposes of barter. The heads were generously coated with an ochre liquid, which the men claimed to be curare. They were passed from hand to hand with some care, for the men jokingly insisted that the merest scratch from their needle-sharp points would be fatal. In fact, since the curare-users have traditionally been enemies of the men of Toototobi, it seemed unlikely that they would have been willing to trade lethal weapons that might later be used against them in warfare.

Yanomami bows are generally about six feet long, a foot or two shorter than the arrows but still much bigger than any of the hunters that use them. The best are made of peach-palm wood, and strung with a plant fibre grown in the gardens. Each hunter makes his own bow. The only other hunting equipment that every man takes with him into the forest is a knife and a bamboo quiver, containing a few spare arrowheads that can be bound on to a prepared shaft with the same fibre, coated with resin, in a matter of seconds. A hunter will usually carry no more than three complete arrows, but the

Taking part in a communal fishing session, a man sweeps a bundle of poisonous vines through the muddy waters of a pond. The poison, which infuses into the water, prevents fish's gills from taking up oxygen and forces the fish to the surface.

spare heads kept in his quiver will allow him to re-use each one many times.

Other substances besides *yakoana* are used in hunting, but their role is magical rather than practical. There is a cultivated plant whose bulb, when chopped and smeared with *urucu* dye on a hunter's face, will lead him to find an armadillo's burrow—or so the Yanomami believe. Bulbs of other, similar plants may be placed inside the hollow end of the arrow shaft into which the head is inserted to ensure successful shooting. Yanomami hunters also respect a taboo on mentioning the names of the game they are going to hunt as they believe this would make them run away.

Many Yanomami groups make use of hunting dogs, and in the yano at Toototobi there were several medium-sized hounds with mottled coats. None looked particularly well-fed, which was hardly surprising since they lived mainly on scraps of fruit or vegetable peelings, but on the other hand few had bald patches or running sores. Sometimes they were taken hunting, but the yano-dwellers informed us regretfully they were usually more of a nuisance than a help, tending to lead the hunter off on false trails and frequently disturbing game by their barking.

Before communal hunts, efforts were sometimes made to improve the animals' performance by a training ritual that involved passing the dogs, to the accompaniment of incantations, through a vine hoop decorated alternately with *urucu* dye and white hawk's down. Someone would then try to persuade the dogs to chase a palm bract dragged on a length of liana, while the hunters used wooden whistles to imitate a tapir's cry. Other people would join in, shouting and waving their bows and arrows, to accustom the dogs to the atmosphere of a hunt. All these encouragements proved of little avail, however, as the performance of the dogs remained mediocre.

Without the help of tracker dogs, the hunters of Toototobi had to rely on their own intimate knowledge of the forest and its animals to bring them success. One day, Catoari, the best hunter in the yano, gave me some useful tips on how to recognize the presence of game. If I spotted bushes that had recently been grazed about two feet from the ground, he said, it meant that a tapir was in the vicinity. What was more, it might well be sleeping nearby, for the animals generally nap after eating well. Peccaries could be detected some way off by their characteristic smell, the grunting and squealing of the piglets, and above all by the loud crunching sound made by their teeth as they fed. The best way of detecting the proximity of monkeys, apart from actually spotting them in the trees, was to look out for traces of eaten fruit or droppings on the ground. When the tracks of an ant-eater were seen to be following an erratic course through the forest, it meant that it was feeding on ants and termite nests, rather than travelling from place to place, and would therefore probably still be nearby.

I came to appreciate just how necessary every scrap of information provided by the environment can be when I spent a day hunting with José, a young man who lived across the yano from us. We left the building at exactly 8 a.m. Besides his waistband and a bead necklace, José had nothing with him but his bow, a knife, three arrows and a quiver. I felt overdressed by con-

A hunter's collection of brightly coloured feathers hangs by his hearth to demonstrate his skill in the chase. Later, the trophies will be stored to keep them safe from the ravages of insects, and brought out on special occasions to be used as body adornments.

trast in my shirt, shorts and tennis shoes. We took a track to the south-west, and walked fast for about an hour without spotting any game. Then José, who carried his bow and arrows slung over his right shoulder, suddenly stopped as something moved off the path to our right. I froze in my tracks. Slowly he lowered his weapon, took aim and fired at a target on the ground that was invisible to me. Then, in no hurry, he strode over to pick up his prey—a bird resembling a russet partridge, with bright red beak and legs. He quickly wrapped it in a leaf parcel, and we passed on through the forest.

We continued walking for the next two and a half hours. During this time, José shot unsuccessfully at a capuchin monkey moving in the tree tops a hundred yards or so off the track, and at a small brown bird that ran across our path. He also shot several times at toucans perched over our heads. These birds are valued highly by the Yanomami for their brilliant red and yellow tail feathers. He called to them with a whistle on four declining notes, but although they came closer to him each of his shots went wide. I began to wonder if his lack of success was due to my presence.

I had almost given up hope of seeing any game bigger than a monkey when without any warning we walked into the middle of a herd of white-lipped peccaries. The pigs scattered noisily in all directions, except for one that stopped in full view about 20 feet away. I could see its bright little eyes staring at us below raised bristles as it hesitated over which way to run. José very slowly raised a broad-bladed arrow to his bow. In a single, steady motion, he notched it to the bowstring, drew and fired. It was a clear hit, and the pig ran off wounded into the forest. I expected José to pursue it at once, but instead he picked up a second arrow and, betraying signs of nervousness, rapidly started to replace its monkey-bone tip with a second big-game head that he took from his quiver. It dawned on me that this was a moment of real danger, for peccaries are known to charge *en masse* when attacked. An enraged herd can trample a man to death in seconds.

Becoming aware of an acrid, pig-like smell, I began to look for a suitable tree to climb in case of danger. But José, who was more cheerful now that he was suitably armed, gave me a quick grin and disappeared into the forest in pursuit of the wounded pig. There were no birds calling in that corner of the forest, and even the insects seemed quieter than usual as I sat there on my own, listening for the crunch of peccary teeth. I was relieved when José returned, even though he came back empty-handed but for the arrow he had shot, which had worked loose and then broken in two as the quarry fled. His shot had been poor, he later confessed, and the animal had not been wounded severely enough to be worth following.

It was now four hours since we had left the yano, and we had paused only to stalk prey. I calculated that we had covered about 10 miles, and were therefore approaching the limit of the territory in which the people of Toototobi normally hunt. Earlier we had passed through at least three abandoned gardens, but now at last the forest was beginning to look totally unaffected by men. The fact that we had had to go so far on a day's hunt was striking evidence of the disadvantage, from the Yanomami's point of view, of staying in the same area for a long time. In the Toototobi region, where our hosts had lived for nearly 20 years, game was evidently becoming scarce.

For an hour we left the track and travelled in a wide circle through virgin forest, but only once came near to adding to our bag. That was when we heard the low whooping of a trumpeter bird, a sound José at once began to imitate faithfully. The bird answered and began to approach us, occasionally interrupting its gentle call with a suspicious squawk. Finally it stepped cautiously out into a ray of sunlight, providing a perfect target. But once again, ill luck dogged our steps. As José raised his bow to shoot, it caught on an unnoticed strand of liana above his head. The slight sound was sufficient to alert the bird, which vanished into the forest at high speed.

Rejoining the hunting track at the point where we had seen the peccaries, we set off home at a cracking pace, pausing only to collect some caterpillars that José spotted in a low palm tree. Inside a nest made of dead leaves we found about 60 large, dark-green larvae, each roughly four inches long. José pulled off their heads one by one, and squeezed out the inedible innards. Wrapping the remains in a palm leaf, we hurried home, arriving back at the yano at four o'clock in the afternoon, exactly eight hours after our departure. Our catch amounted to one partridge and some caterpillars—a painfully small recompense for an entire day's hunting. Yet I was exhilarated by the wildlife I had seen, and pleasantly tired after travelling more than 20 miles on foot without any break to eat.

I was disappointed that no big game had been killed, however, as I was eager to find out how the Yanomami divided up and shared out the animals they killed. I had the chance to put this right a few days later, when word came that Catoari had shot a tapir and was returning into the forest with some of the women to butcher the carcass and share out the meat. I ran to catch up with them, following the track of broken twigs they had left behind.

Together, we moved through the forest for almost two hours before we reached the spot where he had shot the animal. The body lay a few yards farther on, huge and bloated. The butchery began at once. It was a major operation, taking 45 minutes to accomplish. When it was finally completed, the women gathered with baskets lined with palm leaves in which to carry their share. Catoari distributed the meat evenly between them, indulging in much good-natured banter about whose basket could hold a bit more. In all, the tapir provided enough meat to fill seven large baskets; the remaining scraps of offal were thrown to the dogs. Only the head was left behind, its dull eyes staring pig-like into the forest.

Generosity is considered an essential prerequisite for success in hunting. Hunters do not eat the meat of game they have killed themselves, for any man who does so will, the Yanomami believe, be deserted by the hawk spirit which must enter him if he is to thrive in the chase. If they are hunting with other men, they will not even carry their own kills back to the yano, but will give them away to someone else at once. When the group returns to the yano, the recipient will then distribute the meat to his own network of relatives. The original hunter will not go hungry, however, for the man to whom he gave his kill will generally reciprocate by offering in return his own bag.

Because of the rules of hunting etiquette, it would be theoretically possible for a man to live without bothering to hunt at all, as he would always be given meat by others. However, such a man would lose all his prestige in the eyes of his fellows, as well as all respect from the women, to the extent that his wife would probably leave him. Nothing better illustrates the truly communal nature of Yanomami life than this disinterested system of food distribution, in which the provider automatically disposes of everything he kills.

For the Yanomami hunter, the hunt is everything, literally his prime purpose in life, on a level with rearing and defending his children. His masculinity and his pride are bound up with his prowess and his generosity, so that most of his thoughts, plans, dreams and stories revolve around the chase.

# The Most Prestigious Skill

For the Yanomami, the most intense moments of a man's life are spent in the forest, where he goes to track game. Much of his prestige rests on his ability as a hunter. To woo a girl, he will be expected to give presents of meat to her family, and as additional proof of his prowess he will adorn himself with the feathers of birds that he has killed.

The only weapons the Yanomami use are bows and arrows, but these are formidable arms, each much taller than the men who use them. The arrowheads are removable, being attached to cane shafts with fibre. The choice of head depends on the prey. Bamboo is used for large animals,

On a forest track near the yano, a hunter takes aim at a quarry. Like all Yanomami men, he uses an arrow more than seven feet long—bigger than those

a barb of monkey bone for birds, and sharpened palm wood for monkeys.

Within the yano, a man's most common task is preparing or repairing his hunting equipment. He spends even more time putting the weapons to use, however, for all but the oldest men hunt almost every day. They generally set off soon after dawn, to make the most of the coolness of the day, and often spend six hours or more in the forest. After a large kill, the meat is divided among the inhabitants of the yano. Though his family will be given a portion, the successful hunter himself receives no share. His reward lies instead in the generosity he can display to his kinsmen.

used by any other Amazonian Indians. The missile is tipped with a barb of monkey bone, bound on with a length of fibre that is held fast with resin.

Making an arrow, a hunter named Helio carves a hardwood plug (top) with a groove in which the drawstring of the bow will rest. He fits the plug to the butt end of a cane arrow-shaft (bottom), pushing it into the cane's pulpy core and securing it with cotton.

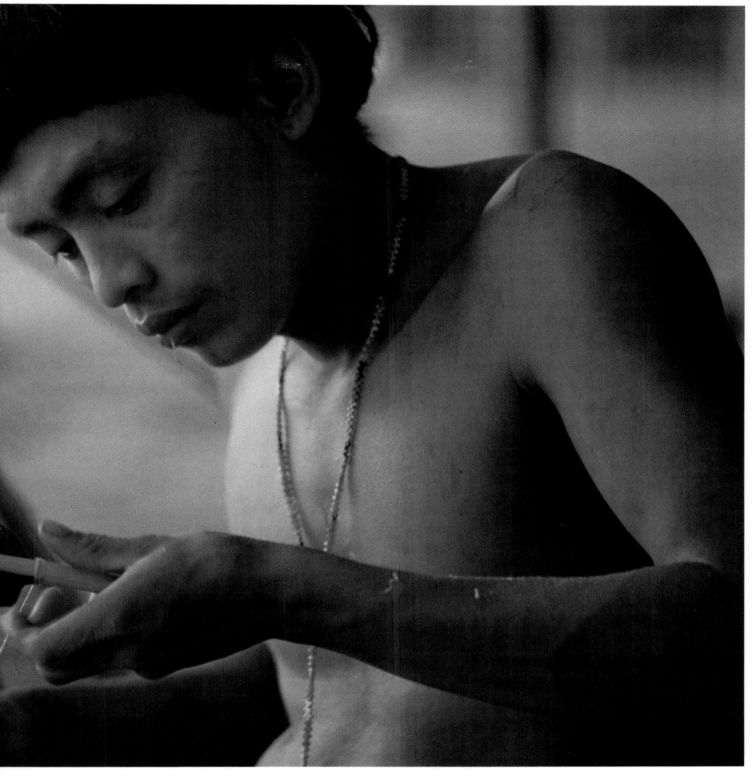

Helio's next step is to fix feathers to the
butt to steady the arrow when it is in
flight. Matching sections of two plumes
from a black curassow are set on
opposite sides of the shaft and bound
into place with additional lengths of cotton.

Sitting on a bark hammock at his hearth, Helio squints along the shaft of a finished arrow to check that it is straight. Arrows frequently warp as a result of use and the prevailing humidity, so hunters must constantly check their weapons to be sure that they will fly evenly. Shafts that are slightly bent can be heated over a fire for a few seconds and flexed back into shape.

Over an open fire in the forest, a hunter bakes a toxic coating on to arrowheads made from palm wood (above). The sticky resin, extracted from the bark of the virola tree, dries and hardens in the heat (right). The heads, which are notched so the tips will break off in the body of the prey, will be used to kill monkeys; the resin acts as a muscle relaxant to make them fall from trees.

**With their bows and arrows clasped ready for action, four hunters hurry along a narrow forest track in search of prey. Usually the Yanomami hunt in**

smaller groups, but when word reaches the yano that big game—such as a herd of wild pigs—is nearby, several hunters will jointly set off in pursuit.

Preparing to return to the yano after a kill, a hunter bends beneath the heavy weight of his quarry—a giant ant-eater. Ant-eaters, which can measure as long as six and a half feet from their snouts to the tips of their bushy tails, provide 30 pounds or more of strong-smelling, slightly bitter meat.

Back in the yano, the ant-eater is skinned on a mat of leaves before butchery. The meat will be shared out around the yano, and the skin discarded.

# *Four* | **Explorers of the Spirit World**

Most mornings at Toototobi, I woke to hear strange noises disturbing the pre-dawn calm of the yano. Sometimes they took the form of a repeated staccato cry, at other times of a monotonous drone, reminiscent of Gregorian plainsong, which reinforced the cathedral-like atmosphere of the yano before sunrise. The sound was so familiar to my hosts that no one paid any attention to it, and it failed to disturb the sleep of the late risers. It was the invocation of one of the yano's shamans, calling down his spirit helpers.

The voice was always male, for only men become shamans. Beyond that basic sexual link, however, there seemed to be little in common among the practitioners of the art. In theory, there is indeed no reason why every adult Yanomami male should not take up shamanism, but in practice only certain individuals feel the call and are willing to undergo the rigours of initiation. At Toototobi, nine of the 20 men in the community were shamans; their ages ranged from the early twenties to 60 or over.

The spirits they were summoning were powerful beings believed by all Yanomami to be one of the principal sources of the illnesses and other misfortunes that befall them. The spirits are at the same time the principal therapeutic agents used to counter such ills, for they can be manipulated by friendly shamans—the healers of the Yanomami world—to cure diseases.

Most of the voices I heard in the morning chill of Toototobi, however, were not at that moment engaged in medicine but were calling down spirits merely for practice, to exercise their skills. At other times shamans may also use their powers to avert storms, to bring success in hunting, to make an individual a good hunter or warrior, or to put to flight spirits sent against the yano by hostile shamans. Alternatively they may in their turn take the offensive and send their own spirits to distant enemy yanos, with the intention of killing children or provoking such catastrophes as the destruction of a plantain crop or the disappearance of a particular type of game.

The inspiration to become a shaman may come in dreams in which the spirits speak to an individual, or else he may experience a claustrophobic

sensation, dimly familiar I am sure to many of us in other forms, in which, when out hunting alone, the surrounding forest seems to be closing in on him and the animals he is hunting laugh crazily at him. Once started on the path, the novice puts himself under the tutelage of one or more established shamans, who initiate him into the mysteries of the spirit world, dosing him with a powdered hallucinogen that is blown up his nostrils through a tube.

During the initiation, which can last as long as eight days, the novice must paint and decorate himself with care. A hearth will be provided for him in an empty section of the yano; his only equipment will be a bark hammock, a pile of wood for his fire, and a gourd of water. Once all the arrangements have been made, his sponsors will take hallucinogens themselves before feeding him with quantities of the drug. They will then invoke the spirits to make them enter the body of the initiate, dancing and singing for several hours to act out the arrival of each one.

The spirits are known as *hekura*, and they take the form of microscopically small Yanomami arriving decorated as though for a feast. Although tiny, they are conspicuous in their bright, festive colours. They fear dirt, and always stay at least a yard above ground level. They often represent animal spirits in miniature human form; yet the Indians also recognize some of them as purely supernatural beings, without direct equivalents in the real world.

The novice will be very frightened by the first confused sensations produced by the hallucinogen, and may run off into the forest, roll around on the ground or, exhausted, faint away. In any case, he will be in an extremely intense emotional state, exacerbated by hunger and isolation. At this stage he will start to see the spirits approaching on a path of light resembling a sunbeam, coming either from the sky or from the distant mountains that the Yanomami believe to lie at the edge of the world.

The long initiation is a profound psychic experience in which the novice's only guidelines for understanding the unfamiliar and frightening sensations are the incessant chants of his initiators, who kneel close to him, fingers pointing to the sky, while they describe in detail each approaching *hekura* and sing the song appropriate to it. The novice is called upon to repeat their chants after them. With their words, his tutors teach him to see.

After his initiation, the novice will be physically weak but he cannot yet afford to relax his efforts to establish contact with the spirits. Among the precautions he must take to ensure that his *hekura* do not abandon him are sexual abstinence, and taboos on hunting and on eating certain foods. After a few weeks, he will undertake his first sessions in shamanism, singing in a low voice and moving very slowly because he is still weak. In time his contact with the spirits will gradually become stronger and his chants will grow in volume. He will have become a true shaman. Henceforth, he will have to take the drug regularly in order to remain master of the sensations he experiences under its influence.

The spirits that the shamans contact are not the only supernatural forces thronging the world of the Yanomami. The supernatural powers fall into two main categories. The first are forces of nature, which may be forest spirits inhabiting specific places—a hill, say, or a thicket—or alternatively spirits of the elements, linked to the rain, the night, clouds and other phenomena; in any case they are hideous to look at and dangerous to meet, for they regard human life as the Yanomami regard game. The second category is composed of forces under human control and these too take two different forms. Some are forces that can be harnessed by sorcery, which any Yanomami can practise and whose tools are the magic plants that all Yanomami grow in their gardens. And there are the *hekura*, under the exclusive control of shamans.

The shaman is the mediator between all supernatural powers, of whatever category, and the yano community. To defeat spirit aggressors, he needs the help of his own *hekura*, contacted through regular use of hallucinogens. The shaman will often dance while chanting to a particular spirit. Both the chant and the dance will identify the spirit he is invoking, and may include imitating the sound and movements of the animal from which the spirit takes its name. Such imitations can be quite realistic. One of the shamans at Toototobi, a 45-year-old called José, was most convincing as an ant-eater, with his arms curved out in front of him and his face contorted into a grimace.

As the shaman dances and chants, he identifies completely with the spirit he is summoning; the Yanomami often use the same term to describe both the spirit and its invoker. In the heightened state of awareness induced by the hallucinogen, the shaman is believed to share the powers credited to his spirit helper. These include supernatural vision, permitting him to see through the flesh of a patient to discover the cause of a disease, as well as the ability magically to cross great distances and an array of supernatural weapons to destroy malevolent spirits or substances.

Each *hekura* has particular skills or abilities associated with the physical attributes of the animal it represents. It is the use to which these may be put, particularly in terms of healing, that guides the shaman's choice of helper. Thus fish *hekura* are called down to spray water over a patient and so lower his temperature, while the spirits of monkeys, which are described by the

A patient suffering from pains in his chest
watches from his hammock as a shaman,
under the influence of hallucinogens, calls
down spirits to help him diagnose and
cure the complaint. Such acts of healing are
the Yanomami shaman's chief social duty.

Yanomami as having "sticky hands" because of their skill in climbing, are often summoned to help extract a pathogen from a patient's body. Each shaman also has certain *hekura* peculiar to himself, given to him by the man who initiated him, with which he is in almost daily contact.

On one occasion when I was sitting by our hearth, the yano was whipped by a sudden strong wind. At once Mateus, who was a shaman as well as our neighbour and host, began to chant. The wind, he told me, was a sign that hostile Yanomami far away were sending a flight of *hekura* to kill children.

In this and similar conversations with shamans, I was impressed by the way in which their discourse flowed unhesitatingly, without any change of expression or attitude, between what we consider the real world and the world of the spirits. Mateus discussed the nature and location of the *hekura* in exactly the same tone of voice he used to describe the animals he hunted and his daily activities in the garden. For the Yanomami, the unity of all life is self-evident, and such subjects as religion, magic and philosophy are not treated as something separate from daily reality.

Within the Yanomami scheme of things, the shamans are a unique, creative force. They are granted status by the community for their ability to become another person, to change personality, to act as the mouthpiece for the otherwise unknown forces at work in the universe. They repay the debt not merely by their efforts as healers and protectors, but also by the part they play in explaining the world to their fellows. Experts in mythology, they alone can interpret the cosmology of the Yanomami, and relate the Indians' own lives to those of the living creatures and spirits with which they believe the universe to be shared. They are the explorers of the spirit world.

Whatever the purposes for which his efforts are intended, the shaman's principal means of access to the spirit world is through hallucinogenic drugs. A shaman needs constant practice to be ready at all times to control the effects of the drug and use it efficiently to call down his *hekura*. Normally only shamans use the hallucinogens. The exception to this rule comes at the end of feasts, when all men and even some of the young boys in a community may be given them. Many of these unaccustomed users get very frightened by their experiences, but others may respond to the sensations and find they have an aptitude for shamanism.

At Toototobi, two main types of drugs, called *yakoana* and *baara*, were used. The first was made from the bark of a tree commonly found in the wild near the Toototobi river. By contrast, *baara*—which is identical to the drug known in Venezuela as *yopo*—was made from the seeds of a plant that did not grow at Toototobi, and so had to be acquired by trade from Yanomami living to the west. Both *yakoana* and *baara* contain a powerful psychoactive substance that produces visual images of geometric patterns and fast shifting colours as well as physical symptoms such as perspiration, dilation of the pupils, involuntary muscular contractions and raising of the blood pressure. Both drugs were frequently taken on their own, but they were also sometimes mixed with two additives known respectively as *ama*—also obtained

## A Drying-Rack for Drugs

The most important of the hallucinogens used by the Yanomami shamans is made from strips scraped from the inner surface of the resinous bark of the *virola* tree. Before crushing the scrapings to a powder that can be inhaled, the shaman must dry them thoroughly. Often he sets them in a basket over a fire, but sometimes he will construct a special rack that allows the sun's heat to do the job.

To prepare such a rack, he binds a branch that has been bent into a rough circle on to a wooden pole, and lashes strips of flexible bark across the hoop. After spreading the *virola* scrapings over this base and securing them with additional strands of bark, he stands the finished rack in the yano's central plaza.

Within a few hours, the scrapings will be paper-dry and ready for grinding into powder. The rack itself, having served its purpose, will be discarded.

**A shaman ties strips of bark to a wood frame.**    **He covers the strips with virola scrapings.**    **A completed parcel dries in the sun.**

from the bark of a tree—and *mashara*, a powder made from dried leaves.

One day, Bruce, Victor and I accompanied Mateus on an excursion into the forest in search of the raw materials for *yakoana*. This commonly used drug, extracted from the bark of the *virola* tree, is used as an arrow poison as well as a hallucinogen; its muscle-relaxant properties make it particularly useful for hunting monkeys, which fall to the ground from the trees when hit by a *yakoana*-tipped arrow. After walking for an hour and a half along narrow hunting trails, we finally found a specimen of the tree some distance off the path. It was tall and slender, with a trunk about two feet in diameter that branched about half way up the tree's full height into three candelabra-like stems. The leaves seemed much attacked by insects and I could see the sky through small holes in them.

Mateus first cut a sliver of bark, which immediately began to ooze little red globules of liquid on its inner side. This confirmed that the resin was rising and the tree therefore in the right condition for the drug to be obtained. He then gathered some wood and soon made a fire, using shavings from a sapling he had cut down as kindling.

Clouds of white smoke rose up through the foliage as Mateus began to cut strips about five feet long from the lowest part of the trunk, peeling them down easily after an initial cut with his machete. He laid the first two over the fire, at which the red liquid began to flow out quite strongly. Taking about a dozen arrow points made of sharpened palm wood from his quiver, he began to scoop up the liquid on his finger and apply it repeatedly to much of the length of the arrowheads. He heated the bark in sections, removing and applying the resin as it emerged, and pausing every five minutes or so to bake on the poison in the heat of the smoke.

He continued this process of applying and heating for an hour, using the resin of five full strips of bark. Then he stuck all the arrowheads point upwards in the ground like a fan and attacked the tree again. This time he removed all the rest of the bark, cutting the strips into three-foot lengths.

The tree, being completely ring-barked, would now die, and it was interesting that, although Mateus said there were plenty more of these trees in the forest, we had had to walk so far to find one. Most of the *virola* trees of this species within a short distance of the yano must have been killed off—another inconvenience for the Yanomami of living in the same place for too long, as the Toototobi community had done.

Mateus next scraped off the pulpy inner coat of the bark, using the blade of his machete. This operation took a further hour, in which time I calculated that he had used roughly six square yards of bark to produce a little over two pounds of wet scrapings. We returned to the yano, where the scrapings were carefully shredded and separated by hand before being laid in a sieve-like basket, which was held over the fire to dry them.

Later I was to see an alternative drying method when a hunter returned from the forest with what looked from a distance like a tennis racket over his shoulder. It turned out to be more of the same scrapings held between pieces of bark stretched across an oval frame. The rack was placed in the ground facing the afternoon sun to obtain the maximum drying effect.

When the peeled bark was crisp, dry and crinkly, it was rolled and then crushed on a clay plate until it was reduced to a coarse powder. Mateus then ground it finely, using a stick as a pestle. He sieved the dust through a fine-mesh basket, and again ground the residue. He scraped the powder, now the colour of red ochre, into a heap in the centre of the clay plate with a feather before sieving and grinding it one more time. As he did so, he explained that making the powder so fine meant that it hurt his sinuses less when inhaled. In all, the six square yards of bark ended up as less than an ounce of snuff.

While Mateus was at work, Helio brought over some strips of grey *ama* bark. He cut these strips into six-inch lengths and, shaping them into little canoes—I thought at first, naively, that they were toys for the children—burnt them to ashes on a carefully swept section of the earth floor. Delicately scooped into the mortar, the ashes were then ground in their turn. The very fine, slate-grey ash was then sieved directly on to the red *yakoana* on the clay plate and the two powders were swept into one heap with the feather. Some previously prepared *baara* powder, a dark brown in colour, was added to the mixture from a container. When the mixing was complete, Mateus tested the results, inhaling a small pinch; so did every male around. The blend was pronounced good and scooped into the container for future use.

A couple of days later, Mateus obligingly advised us that he was about to embark on a shamanistic session with the aid of this strong mixture of three

A shaman gathers handfuls of leaves from a fragrant plant growing in his garden. When the plant's leaves (inset, right) have been dried, they will be crushed to a fine powder and mixed with a potent hallucinogenic snuff to make the mixture smell good and to ease the discomfort of its inhalation.

hallucinogens. In preparation, he had already painted his entire body carefully with *urucu* dye, and had placed a feather decoration in his left armband.

As we watched, he poured a small heap of the powder on to the same clay plate on which it had been mixed. Then he took down his powder tube—a three-foot section of hollowed arrow-cane capped at one end by the casing of a palm-fruit stone shaped to serve as a funnel and stuck on with resin. Placing a pinch of the powder in the open end of the tube, he flicked it so that the drug spread evenly down the barrel. He inserted the capped end in his left nostril. His small, blond son, Abel, squatted down facing him and gave a short, sharp puff into the open end of the tube. A cloud of dust rose around Mateus's head; the rest of the powder entered his nose. This operation was repeated five more times through both nostrils, with pauses of a minute or two between inhalations. Mateus became progressively more uncomfortable. spitting, slapping his sides, shaking and stroking his head, and shifting his position from one foot to the other.

At that point Abel got up and strolled away, no longer interested in what was to him a routine event. Putting the plate and the tube aside, Mateus sat for a while in contemplation. Then, slowly, he began to sing and to sway from side to side. Soon he was on his feet, chanting and stamping, his arms outstretched and his eyes glazed and directed upwards. Covering always the same piece of ground, he moved back and forth, singing a whole series of different short refrains, each one the song of a particular spirit. He stopped after 20 minutes and squatted on his haunches for a short rest, slapping himself, passing his hands through his hair and grinning broadly at no one in particular. Then he fetched two arrows and danced with them for a time.

He was in another world, apparently transported and oblivious to his surroundings and yet able in an instant to return to earth. His co-ordination was perfect; he was steady on his feet and never staggered or faltered. He could pick up things and place them accurately with no difficulty, and he never bumped into any of the many upright posts past which he was parading. At one moment, a tame guan that lived in his hearth as a pet flew down from the pole on which it roosted to stand in his way and caw at him. Without breaking the rhythm of his chant, he picked up the powder tube and hit the bird with it. Yet when I looked into his face or caught his eye, I knew that it was not any earthly creature he was laughing at or talking to.

After about an hour, Abel returned and blew three more doses of the drug into his father's nostrils. Immediately Mateus was galvanized into faster and more energetic action. The rhythm of his chant increased, and his dancing became more and more animated.

After a time, I began to recognize some standard positions that I had seen other shamans adopt at various stages in their repertoires. First he struck a pose with one arm raised upwards, the finger pointing; then he brought the raised arm down violently with a loud, shouted "thaiee . . ." to imitate the flashing of lightning. Next, squatting on his haunches, he began to hop about with his arms outstretched, crying "heeee, heeee" in a loud voice to mimic the call of a vulture. At other times he drew the index finger of his right hand

# A Shaman at Work

Besides treating any individual ailments caused by malevolent forest spirits or by human sorcerers, the Yanomami shaman is responsible for protecting his community against supernatural spirit helpers that have been dispatched by distant and hostile shamans. To tackle these threats, he must first activate his own spirit helpers—described by shamans as tiny creatures in human form but generally having the characteristics of particular animals. Because such spirits have an antipathy to dirt of any kind, the shaman will wash himself carefully, decorate his body and put on his most beautiful feathers. He then inhales a powdered hallucinogen, and, as the drug takes effect, summons his helpers to him.

The shaman may invoke several spirit helpers, each selected for its ability to cope with different aspects of the task in hand. For healing, he may choose a spirit with the cooling properties of a fish or the agility of a monkey, but for battle against supernatural adversaries he opts for the aggressive qualities of a special spirit associated with the machete.

Under the spell of this spirit, the shaman takes up his own machete. Acting out the conflict, he chants and dances, hacking at the air to simulate driving the enemy from the yano and thereby restoring the well-being of the community.

**Antonio, headman of the Toototobi yano, grimaces (above) as he inhales a powdered hallucinogen administered through a tube (right). His tobacco wad rests on one foot; he will replace it in his mouth after inhaling.**

Dazed by the drugs he has taken, Antonio becomes possessed by his spirit-helpers (below). Under their influence, he begins to dance (right), his postures reflecting the personality of the spirit he has chosen to help him. He grows increasingly animated, and finally raises his machete to scatter the supernatural forces threatening the yano.

out of his clenched left fist, making an easily recognizable gesture to indicate shooting arrows; during this part of his dance he identified with a warlike spirit associated with arrows, summoned to improve the shaman's marksmanship. Between the different phases, he would rest briefly, his hands on his knees and his head hanging down, or else merely continue the endlessly varied chant accompanied by exaggerated rhythmic steps, placed lightly and delicately at the last moment.

After about two and half hours, the influence of the drug seemed to wane, and Mateus brought the performance to an end. He put all his equipment away carefully and tidily, then went back to his hammock, where he chatted to his family as though his trance had been the most natural thing in the world. For him, of course, it was.

As far as I was concerned, one of the most interesting aspects of Mateus's behaviour—and of that of his fellow shamans when under the influence of drugs—was the apparently total mastery that he had throughout over his actions. The snuff they inhaled was an extremely potent hallucinogen of a type that, even when taken under controlled medical conditions in the developed world, might well be frighteningly disorientating. Yet the Yanomami shamans never seemed to suffer any discomfort other than a slight discharge from the nostrils and some short-lived physical irritation just after inhaling the powder. Thereafter, all the sensations accompanying their energetic chanting and parading appeared pleasurable and, above all, controlled.

I also noted that regular use of the drug had apparently not damaged their health in the slightest. Even the older shamans, who had been taking hallucinogens perhaps once a week all their adult lives, seemed quite as fit, strong and intellectually alert as their fellows.

I have always considered the indiscriminate use of drugs as a serious social problem in the modern industrial world. The Yanomami approach to hallucinogens, however, is a completely different matter. By providing a philosophical framework within which the experience can be understood and assimilated, and controlled conditions for the drugs' use, the Yanomami seem to have avoided any problems of abuse. In fact, this is an area where the Indians are the experts and we are the novices. The psychological experiments which the shamans are constantly making in the most serious way are directly equivalent to, and arguably well in advance of, our own research.

The main social function of the shamans is curing the sick. Taking a supernatural view of the causes of illness, the Yanomami naturally turn to those with transcendental power to cure them. This attitude does not mean, however, that the Yanomami fail to take account either of hygiene or of healing medicines. True, their attitude towards sanitation is very different from that of the urban, industrial world. To defecate, for example, the Indians use certain selected spots in the forest, off the hunting trails and well away from water supplies. They regard the idea of using a single communal hole for the disposal of excrement as disgusting, with good reason as in the rain forest the concentration of bacteria that would develop round a single, unflushable

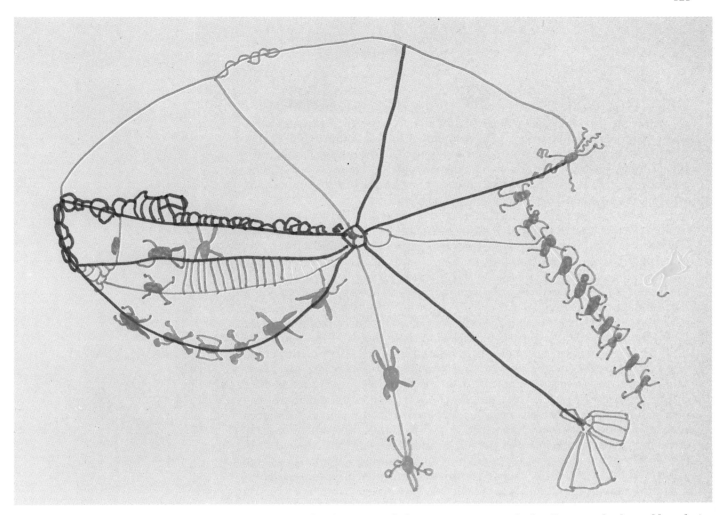

toilet area would be extremely unhealthy. Similarly, they regard the Western habit of blowing the nose into a handkerchief with abhorrence—and
here again, their views are sound. In the tropical rain forest where micro-
organisms breed with extreme speed, the collection of germs in a single
disposable packet would be far more dangerous than the Indians' way of
never concentrating dirt in one place.

For the relief of familiar ailments, the Yanomami make use of an array of
medicinal plants. To alleviate the effects of snake bites, for instance, they rub
the wound with the leaves of the jacaranda tree; other substances, including
the bark of the cinchona tree from which quinine is derived, are used for a
variety of common complaints that include malaria, eye infections, vomiting
and upset stomachs. At Toototobi, where the missionaries had provided
access to imported medicaments, the traditional forest pharmacopoeia had
been supplemented, and to some extent supplanted, by manufactured drugs,
which the Yanomami accepted easily into their own range of healing aids.

Such practical medicines play a relatively small part, however, in the Yanomami's treatment of diseases. The therapy chosen in most cases is treatment by shamans, which is more often psychosomatic in its emphasis. The
shamans' first job is diagnosis. The Yanomami recognize four main causes of

**Asked to illustrate what he could see during his trances, a young shaman produced this drawing of his vision. The small red and purple figures represent spirits responding to his invocation. The straight lines are the rays of light along which the spirits travel from their yano in the sky to the shaman's own yano, indicated by the bow-shaped object in the bottom right-hand corner.**

disease: the action of *hekura* sent by hostile shamans, ailments caused by the sorcery of an ill-wisher using magic plants, attack by forest spirits, and harm caused to a man by injury done to a particular animal in some distant part of the forest, considered to be his double with whom he shares a part of his destiny. If the animal twin, which may be deer, a tapir, a monkey, a bird, or any other forest creature, is injured by a hunter, then its Yanomami counterpart will fall ill; and when it dies, its human *alter ego* will die too.

The three other causes of disease are all the result of direct aggression against the afflicted individual. In the case of attack by forest spirits, the invader is a force of nature, whose assaults are unpredictable and can only be thwarted by prompt action on the part of a friendly shaman and his *hekura*. The other two causes—the action of hostile *hekura*, and sorcery—are both the product of human malice; only shamans can send *hekura*, however, while any Yanomami can practise sorcery.

The raw materials of sorcery are near at hand, in the form of plants grown in nearly every family's garden plot. Normally the bulbs of the plants are used. They may be finely chopped or powdered and used either on their own or mixed with other ingredients such as wild plants, insects or animal hairs. Most people carry a few such mixtures, wrapped in packages hidden in their quivers, when they go to a feast, and they will try to direct them at individuals against whom they bear a grudge, perhaps because of sexual jealousy, a real or imagined insult or a suspected theft. To do this, they will attempt to place the charm on the enemy's person, or in his food or tobacco wad. One favoured method is to cast the powder at an individual while he is asleep. Sorcery of this sort is often blamed for illnesses suffered after feasts involving allied yanos, though rarely for deaths. A more serious form of sorcery is employed by warriors against enemy yanos. Sneaking up on their enemies, they will attempt to strike an isolated individual, travelling through the forest or working in the gardens, with a palmwood dart to which the magic plants have been attached by a piece of raw cotton. The victim of such an attack is generally expected to weaken and die within a few days.

An experienced shaman can identify each of the four disease sources by using his drug-induced supernatural vision to spot a tell-tale sign within the patient's body. The Yanomami refer to such a sign as a "mark"—the same term they use to refer to the imprint left by a dog's teeth or by a knife wound. The mark of an attack by hostile *hekura* sent by enemy shamans, for example, is a small cross with curved arms inside the victim's throat, which causes difficulty in breathing and can lead to suffocation. Disorders caused by forest spirits are marked by what the Indians describe as a tangled loop of red-hot cotton across the chest, showing itself in the form of a fever. A victim of sorcery will experience a burning sensation that the healing shaman will be able to see as sparks of fire within the body; while the distinguishing feature of an injury resulting from the wounding of a person's animal double is a tiny arrowhead inside the body, causing acute, localized pain.

Detecting such pathogens is, for the Yanomami, an exercise that requires years of shamanistic experience. In addition, the shaman must be sensitive

After several exhausting hours of diagnosis, a shaman strokes the head of a feverish child to draw out his sickness. Throughout the whole curing process, a close bond exists between the shaman and his patient, creating the strong sense of security that is fundamental to all Yanomami healing.

to the mood of his fellows, for the diagnosis that he comes to may be affected by his group's political situation. If he settles on sorcery as the cause of the disease, he will bring about conflict between the sufferers and the group he accuses. As a result, such accusations are never made against members of one's own yano. They are often made against individuals from neighbouring yanos, after feasts, and can lead to fights, though almost never to serious injury. More serious accusations of sorcery leading to deaths are normally only levelled at distant and rarely encountered groups.

To trace the pathogen, a shaman will take several doses of hallucinogen and start to dance and chant to summon his *hekura*. During this phase, he often asks the patient questions about the onset of the disease and its symptoms. Once he has used this information and the insight provided by his *hekura* to complete the diagnosis, he can proceed to the appropriate cure. This will usually include chants and dances designed to summon spirits with the necessary powers to drive out the malady. At intervals the shaman will break off his performance to work on the patient's body, massaging it vigorously and ending each phase of treatment with a clap of the hands and a throwing gesture, indicating that the illness is being ejected. Sometimes the shaman will run wildly around the yano, acting out a psychic drama in which the *hekura* he has summoned hunt down the forest spirit responsible for the illness or fight pitched battles with the enemy *hekura* blamed for its onset. The performance will in any case end with the extraction of the pathogen. Most shamans simply mime this, but a small number of more powerful shamans capable of summoning the *hekura* of a particular bird, the yellow-rumped cacique, are able to vomit up some object similar to the supposed pathogen—which may be a tangle of cotton or the leaves of a magic plant—and produce it before the admiring spectators.

At Toototobi, several shamans would sometimes work together to treat a patient. This was especially true when shamans from another yano were visiting, providing an opportunity for the local healers to learn the songs and dances associated with other *hekura* as well as to benefit from a second opinion on the malady, much as Western doctors might call in specialist consultants for difficult cases.

A particularly dramatic incident occurred when José, the headman of a yano a dozen miles to the south, was visiting the Toototobi yano. During his stay the small son of Jorge, a son-in-law of the headman Antonio, became ill. The seven-year-old showed signs of fever; some time previously he had been treated by the missionaries for malaria.

Mateus and a second local shaman, known as Pelé, joined the visitor to cure the sick child. One by one they inhaled doses of *yakoana*. As they worked themselves into the proper healing state, they generated a tremendous volume of noise, emitting shouts, yells and screams in alternation with rhythmic grunting and clucking and more conventional chanting sounds. After ascertaining the patient's symptoms and how they had developed, they concentrated hard to visualize the pathogen causing the fever. Eventually they all came to the conclusion that the boy's illness had been caused by shamans from the Paduari river region some 80 miles to the south-west, who had sent *hekura* to steal his soul.

At first the three shamans searched for the lost soul and its kidnappers around the yano, and ran about the plaza, calling out to one another. From time to time, one would adopt the manner of an animal *hekura*, faithfully mimicking the agile movements of a spider monkey. They then took the child from his hammock and carried him at a run around the building to protect him from further, possibly fatal attacks.

Finally they succeeded in finding the enemies' tracks. The next stage was to hunt them down. They inhaled further doses of *yakoana* and, summoning all their *hekura*, sent them in pursuit, meanwhile vividly miming the action that was taking place. They simulated the drama of catching up with the enemy, firing magic arrows at them and suffering painful counter-attacks.

The scene culminated with the shamans rescuing the soul and returning it to the child. The business of removing the symptoms of the sickness then got under way. For several hours, the three men surrounded the small hammock in which the boy lay. From time to time, one of them would lean down to rub the small body gently from head to foot, dragging the sickness out of his system before hurling it away with a great roar. Sometimes the three would work together to extract the little cross left in the boy's throat by the enemy *hekura*; at other times they divided, and one would work on the body while the other two kept up a low background chant.

Eventually the child revived sufficiently to sit up and take some plantain soup. Subsequently his condition improved steadily and he recovered completely from the attack. Meanwhile, the shamans, exhausted by their efforts, went back to their hearths. But the yano continued to buzz with talk about the incident. It was generally agreed that the inhabitants were living through dangerous times and that there were many enemy spirits about, which the yano's own shamans would have to make extra efforts to keep at bay.

The performance and its successful conclusion left me with food for thought about the relative effectiveness of Indian and Western medicine. Certainly the fact that the Yanomami consider most diseases to be of supernatural origin does not mean that as healers they are ineffective. A growing body of biomedical research indicates the importance of the patient's mental state in treating even such intractable conditions as cancer. It seems that the faith a patient has in the regimen he is subjected to and the relationship he has with his doctor can often be as important as the medication he receives.

Seen in this light, the shaman's ability to explain a disease and to act out its cure symbolically is very effective medicine indeed. By releasing the patient's stress and anxieties, he provides the climate in which the body's own healing mechanisms can function at their best, and so greatly increases the chances of a successful cure.

## *A Day in the Life of* **Tiago**

The nights are cool in Toototobi, and for two or three hours before dawn recumbent figures shivered and stirred fitfully in their hammocks under the sheltered perimeter of the yano. From time to time a woman rose to fan one of the fires that burned in each family's hearth. As the circle of sky that roofed the central clearing slowly lightened from black to the pale, translucent blue of the forest dawn, the yano's oldest resident, Tiago, opened his eyes, glanced sleepily around the hearth he shared with his young wife and three children, and then lay back in his hammock, half way between sleep and waking as he waited for the start of a new day.

The old man had been given the Portuguese name Tiago by the missionaries; his Yanomami neighbours knew him as Maka Maka. Nobody knew his exact age, for the Yanomami keep no record of birthdays, but his appearance and his memories of past events indicated that he was well past his 60th year. He had been born on the far side of the Parima Massif in Venezuelan Yanomami territory, where he spent the early years of his life in a yano near the headwaters of the Orinoco river. His father died while he was still a child, and he crossed the range with his mother to live with relatives in Brazil. So it was that Tiago first came to the community in whose company he still found himself some 50 years later.

In the intervening half-century, great changes had affected the group. Through Tiago's adolescence and the first stages of his adult life, they moved every five years or so, when the gardens began to lose their fertility, heading gradually southwards down the Toototobi river. The population of the community grew, and on two occasions they fissioned as groups of families departed to set up yanos of their own. As their migration progressed, the Indians came into hostile contact with neighbours to the east and west. Tiago still bore the scar of an arrow wound received in one of the raids that ensued before harmony was restored.

The Toototobi people had their first contact with non-Indians when Tiago was an adolescent. The intruders were Brazilian prospectors who started a measles epidemic among the Indians and deliberately poisoned several Yanomami in revenge for the loss of some goods before fleeing the territory in fear of retaliation. Lasting contact was not established until the Toototobi mission was founded in 1962. In the same year, Tiago and his group moved to their present home near the mission, where they had stayed ever since.

Physically, Tiago retained the strength and agility of a much younger man. He could still shin up and down tall trees to collect palm fruits and honey. Mentally, he was relaxed and at ease with the world. In Yanomami society, the old are always cared for affectionately by their family until death, so he had no cause to feel insecure. Alert and humorous, he took a delight in clowning, and at feasts it was not unusual to find him decked out in a grass skirt or pretending to be bald by putting a calabash upside down over his bushy black hair.

His present wife, who lay in the adjoining hammock, was a woman some 30 years his junior. Given the name Lolita by the missionaries, she was his third partner. His first wife had died many years before; her successor, Teresa, had lived with him for 15 years and provided him with two children, before Tiago decided to marry Lolita, her younger sister—a fairly common occurrence among the Yanomami. He subsequently agreed to let Teresa go when a young bachelor's father asked him to give her to his son. Teresa's second husband, Jonas, had taken her to live in a yano five hours' journey downstream. The couple were currently visiting Toototobi, and were staying as Tiago's guests at the next hearth.

Tiago's two daughters by his previous wives were both by now grown women with husbands of their own. One lived in Jonas's yano, but the other had remained at Toototobi. Her spouse was Tiago's principal provider of meat, for the old man rarely went out hunting any more and when he did it was usually in search of easy prey— armadillos, for instance, that could with comparatively little effort be smoked out of their holes. Thus he could spend much of the day in his hammock, surrounded by the younger children that Lolita had borne him.

Half an hour or more after he had awakened, Tiago left his hammock for the first time to fetch some pieces of papaya from the pot in which they had been stored overnight. He handed slices of the bland yellow fruit to a small flock of youngsters—among them some of his own children and grandchildren—who had gathered around him. Then he climbed back into his hammock, and the young people—having eaten the fruit and tidily thrown the skins away outside the yano—swarmed over him, chattering affectionately.

The first three hours of Tiago's day were uneventful. While the younger men went off to hunt in the forest, he

**The yano's oldest resident relaxes with some of his children and grandchildren on his hammock.**

128

**Tiago does his bit to keep the yano clean.**

was freed by his age to lie dozing in his hammock. In that time he did nothing more energetic than straighten an arrow or two—a hunter's habit that Yanomami men, however old, never lose—and play with the children, with whom he was a particular favourite. Meanwhile, Lolita had swept the floor and put some food to cook over the hearth; then she too returned to her hammock, taking her unweaned son with her.

At mid-morning Tiago helped himself to his first real meal of the day. The previous day, a hunter had killed one of the large, beaver-like rodents known as capybara, and every hearth in the yano had received a share of its soft-textured, fatty flesh. Pieces of the meat were boiling in a blackened aluminium pot over the fire. Using a piece of wood as a fork, Tiago scooped out some meat into a calabash and searched in the cooking liquid until he came up with a piece of manioc. Then he carried the food back to his hammock and ate it from the calabash, using his fingers.

After a lengthy rest, Tiago again stirred himself to clear away some dog excrement befouling the ground outside his hearth. Picking up a small piece of plantain skin, he scraped the dirt on to the blade of his machete before transferring it to a palm leaf that served as a dustpan. He carried the leaf outside the yano and deposited

it on a rubbish dump at the forest's edge. Keeping the yano clean is the business of all its residents, and in the course of the day both Tiago and Lolita made several such trips as part of their housekeeping.

Few other chores disturbed Tiago's peace for the rest of the morning. The calm of the yano was broken only twice—once when a small bird got caught under the roofing, providing the children with a target for some noisy hunting practice, and once when two visitors, with their faces painted bright red and their heads covered with white down, strode into the building and made their way to the hearth of the headman. They had come from a yano half a day's walk away upstream, and word soon circulated that they were bringing an invitation to a funerary feast to be held there in a few days' time. Afterwards, Antonio, the headman, addressed the yano at large to confirm this fact, and a general discussion ensued. Tiago joined in to assure waverers that, although the rainy season had begun, the journey to the other yano would not be too difficult. "The route is not

**He adjusts the rack on which meat is smoking over the hearth.**

found a heap of papaya picked that morning by Lolita and left for the taking. Choosing four fruits, he set them in his basket, and then decided to pick some plantain for good measure. When his basket was full, he lifted it on to his back and secured it by means of an attached sling of flexible bark, which he passed around his forehead. Bending forward to counterbalance the load, he slowly made his way back to the yano, where he dropped the basket at his wife's feet.

He set out from the yano again almost at once, but this time he went into the forest in search of building poles; he needed to finish the roof covering his hearth. Scanning the undergrowth for young trees of a suitable size, he quickly found a sapling that served his purpose, and in just two minutes he had felled it with a succession of machete blows. As the tree fell, a small avalanche of twigs and dead leaves, detached from the surrounding vegetation, all but buried him. Recovering his machete from the debris, he set off in search of other suitable candidates. Within 20 minutes he had cut three poles, each measuring about 12 feet long. Carrying them over

**Tiago carries plantain back from the garden.**

so bad," he insisted. "Just a little water. Don't worry! I'm the only one who will fall in."

When the excitement caused by the visitors' invitation had subsided, Tiago's mind turned again to food. There was still plenty of meat in the hearth as a result of the previous day's kill. In addition to the stew in the pot, Tiago had set a whole capybara leg to smoke on a rack above the fire, and from time to time he adjusted the rack and turned the meat so that it would cure evenly. Fruit, however, was in short supply, so he decided to make a trip to the garden.

Taking with him his machete and carrying basket, he set off briskly on the five-minute walk. In his plot, he

**Poles from the forest will be used for roofing.**

**Holding a bar of soap impaled on a stick, Tiago washes his eldest son in the river.**

his shoulder, he made his way back to the yano again.

There he rewarded himself for his efforts with another meal of capybara meat, accompanied this time by manioc bread, which he held in the same hand as the meat to form an open sandwich. To finish the meal, he cut one of the papaya fruits from the garden into sections, and shared it with his eldest son—a nine-year-old called Adilio—and one of his daughters, who had been playing with the other children in the central plaza. He wiped his hands on a nearby post, belched contentedly, and settled back into his hammock for a siesta.

The sun was already casting slanting shadows in the yano's central plaza when he awoke and announced to the world at large that he was going down to the river to bathe. Picking up a piece of soap provided by the missionaries, he speared it on the end of a stick—a substitute for a soap dish—and set off with Adilio.

When the two companions reached the water's edge, they found that the Toototobi river had burst its banks

overnight, as a result of heavy rains up in the hills, and was swelling in lazy eddies up to the forest's edge. Tiago splashed around in the overflow water for a few minutes, then set about thoroughly washing himself with the soap. Next he turned his attention to Adilio, and carefully soaped him from head to toe. Although Tiago did not associate personal hygiene with health, he—like all Yanomami—appreciated the aesthetic attraction of a clean body, and bathed every day.

A mid-afternoon calm pervaded the yano when the two returned home. Tiago went back to his hammock to devote himself to some minor chores. Taking a handful of twined vegetable fibres, he expertly plaited them together to form a strong length of cord about five feet long. Taking up a bamboo quiver, he wrapped the cord round it in a loop so he could hang the container round his neck while hunting—for no matter how old a hunter might be, he never loses pride in his equipment.

Next, Tiago crouched down to perform one of the

least pleasant but inescapable daily routines of yano life—removing chigoes from his feet. These tiny, burrowing insects infest the compound's earth floor, where they eagerly await the opportunity to transfer themselves to the flesh of its inhabitants, both human and canine. Besides causing irritation by their own presence, female chigoes use human or animal skin as an incubation bed for their eggs, which can prolong the victim's discomfort. To combat the pest, Tiago picked up a seven-foot-long arrow. Resting its shaft against one raised leg, he used the head to dig out egg-sacs from the flesh of one of his toes. As each sac came out, he took it in his fingers and cracked it between his teeth, then spat it out. This practice, which the Yanomami call "taking revenge on the chigoes", prevents the eggs from hatching.

Once he had satisfied himself that all the sacs had been removed from his feet, Tiago, who was still feeling energetic, picked up his machete once more and made his way to the cleared area that lay between the yano and the surrounding forest. Keeping this area free of weeds is primarily a job for the older folk, because it re-

An arrow serves as a scalpel to remove chigoes.

The afternoon is a good time to catch up on sleep.

132

**The old man shins up a pole to do some roofing.**

quires less effort than hunting. Yet nobody in the yano would have dreamt of putting pressure on Tiago, or indeed on anyone else; individuals went out weeding only when the mood took them. Using the blade of his machete to cut off the plants at the roots, Tiago spent the better part of an hour clearing a patch of ground several hundred square feet in extent. After throwing the dead vegetation on to a rubbish heap, he returned to his hearth, to find that Lolita had gone out to the garden to collect firewood. Tired after what had been by far the hardest job of the day, he retired to his hammock for much of the next hour. At one point he got up and strolled over to a relative's hearth to chat about the forthcoming feast. He was greeted warmly and given a snack of manioc bread and plantain soup.

The sun was slanting low over the roof of the yano when Lolita returned with her load, which she left outside the yano. It was a fine evening, and almost all the women and children had deserted the yano to go down

to the river and bathe. Lolita decided to join them with her three youngsters. Typically, Yanomami husbands and their wives go their own ways for much of the day, each doing many of their daily tasks alone or in the company of others of their own sex.

Left to himself, Tiago decided to do some work on the roof above his hearth. Before shinning up one of the poles to start the job, he loosely bound a length of flexible bark round his feet. This loop helped to prevent him from slipping by exerting friction on the pole when he gripped it between his feet. After pulling up some ready-prepared sections of thatch, Tiago then carefully bound them into place on the overhanging eaves with further lengths of twined liana. Then he slid down a pole back to earth, and returned to lie in his hammock.

He spent the next hour sleepily watching the children at play in the plaza, bestirring himself only to chat with one of the visitors who had arrived that morning about a kinsman who lived in the stranger's yano. When Lolita and the three children returned from bathing in the river, Tiago made his way back to the cooking pot in search of his evening snack—the fourth of the day. The

**Lolita mixes ash from the hearth into a tobacco wad for Tiago.**

whole family in turn helped themselves to more of the capybara meat, and also to plantains that had been left to roast in the embers of the fire.

While the rest of his family was still eating, Tiago washed down his food with a drink of water, which he scooped with his gourd from an aluminium pot, refilled each day from the river by Lolita. Then he set about preparing for the approaching night. He hung the cooking pot, which still contained some meat for the next day, high on the yano wall where it would be out of reach of the dogs. He tightened the ropes that secured his hammock to the roof supports, and used a basket to collect the rubbish that had accumulated around the fire in the course of the day. He had earlier asked Lolita to prepare a new tobacco wad for him, and now she duly did so, dipping the tobacco leaves in water and turning them in white ash from the hearth before rolling them into a shape to fit the space between Tiago's lower lip and teeth. Mixed with the tobacco, the ash gives the wad a peppery flavour that is cherished by the Yanomami. Tiago took the wad from Lolita and tested it. Pleased with its taste, he watched the last sunlight drain rapidly from the darkening sky.

As they prepared for sleep, families all around the yano added extra wood to their fires, and the flaring embers pinpricked the gathering gloom with light. Jonas, who had spent the day hunting unsuccessfully in the forest, had returned to his hearth, and for a while Tiago and he gossiped from their hammocks about the day's activities while the children played around them.

Growing tired, Tiago lay back in his hammock and closed his eyes. It had been a quiet day, but then, except at times of feasting, all his days now moved at a leisurely pace. Placidly he listened to the conversations of the youngsters, giggling as they traded jokes and gossip across the yano. With his family grouped around him and his place in the community assured, there was little to disturb his rest. Gradually the talk and the laughter died away, until only faint murmurs from distant hearths intruded upon the sounds of the jungle night. Warmed by the fire's glowing embers, Tiago slowly drifted into a deep and carefree sleep.

After dark, Tiago chats with his neighbours before sleeping.

# *Five* | **A Wider World of Friends and Foes**

From time to time the peace of the yano at Toototobi was disturbed by the arrival of outsiders. Usually the visitors turned out to be familiar individuals from nearby communities, often bearing invitations to feasts, and as such they would be greeted warmly. There was always a moment of tension when newcomers first entered the building, however, for the attitude of the residents to strangers was generally one of suspicion.

Such caution is typical of the way in which the Yanomami regard anyone outside their own community. Every yano is potentially self-sufficient in food and material goods, and, ideally if not always in reality, its members seek to marry within it. As a result, the inhabitants of each yano see themselves as residents of an independent, sovereign unit, protecting its own exclusive territory by means of a deterrent show of hostility towards other groups. Because no political force exists in the Indians' world to intervene in local disputes and guarantee the autonomy of each community, every yano must protect itself and defend its own interests.

In practice, however, no yano can stand alone against the rest of the world, so alliances become necessary to maintain a balance of power. Just as the families making up any one yano are linked by a system of economic give-and-take based on marital ties, so the yanos themselves form part of larger social groupings made up of separate communities bound to one another by political and ceremonial bonds. Such alliances may develop either between splinter groups that are formed when a yano splits as a result of population growth, or when two previously unrelated groups come into contact and establish a friendship through trade and intermarriage. It is from within such a network that each community invites guests to attend feasts or, in times of conflict, to join with them in warrior raids.

At Toototobi the network linked five separate yanos. Besides the group with whom we were staying were two communities that had fissioned from

it in the course of the past 40 years and a couple of groups that had come in from outside. To the north, east and west of this relatively stable axis lived other Yanomami with whom relations oscillated constantly between long periods of conflict and times of uneasy co-existence that had failed to culminate in a permanent alliance.

The brunt of the Toototobi community's suspicions fell on Indians coming from beyond the immediate network of yanos. Like all Yanomami, they divided humankind into four categories. Into the first of these divisions fall fellow-residents of the same yano, thought of as friends. Then there are "guests"—members of allied yanos who, despite being outsiders, might be invited to feasts. Although people in this category are regarded with a certain mistrust, efforts are made to remain on friendly terms with them. The third category—"enemies"—includes all other known Yanomami from outside the network of allied yanos; the fourth, "those we do not see", is a comprehensive category that includes all the distant Yanomami communities they have heard of but have never contacted.

From people in the third and fourth categories the Yanomami always expect hostility. Their apprehensions find expression in a state of permanent potential warfare, designed to maintain the autonomy of each yano. Such mutual enmity generally takes the form of a show of simulated ferocity and verbal bravado, to which occasional outbursts of real violence lend credibility. Actual raids leading to deaths are relatively rare. Yet the Indians talk incessantly about making and receiving attacks, both physical and magical. The idea of warfare is intrinsic to Yanomami society; but that does not mean that the Indians spend their time engaged in actual hostilities. In general, the warrior raids that have so obsessed some Western observers are for the Yanomami only one of the means, and on no account the most important one, of countering the real or supposed hostility of other communities. Skirmishes in the spirit world matter far more than physical violence, and many more deaths are attributed by the Indians to hostile magic than to enemy arrows.

Certainly I experienced only hospitality from the Yanomami. Protected by Bruce's long association with the Indians and the fictional kinship consequently extended to us, Victor and I were made to feel very much at home. Our doings were a source of constant amusement to our hosts, who found our behaviour quite as incongruous as theirs had at first seemed to us. Soon we both had nicknames. Victor was known as "the tapir", a beast linked in Yanomami mythology to thunder, for his deep, rumbling laugh; my own sibilant chuckle won me the sobriquet of "the tortoise" because, I was told, it sounded like the hiss a tortoise makes as it retreats into its shell.

Our visit was well-timed to show us the more welcoming aspects of Yanomami life, for we arrived at the tail end of the dry season, when the last of the plantain harvest was being gathered. It was a period of exceptional abundance. Besides the plantains, manioc was readily available, and peach-palm fruit was plentiful in the abandoned gardens. Conditions for travelling were excellent: the rivers were low and the forest paths were dry. It was the season for feasting *par excellence*.

For the Yanomami, feasts are an opportunity to demonstrate the generosity of the hosts towards allied yanos. The procedure followed at Toototobi was always roughly the same, being closely defined by tradition. First, messengers would be sent to another yano to invite the guests, who might number just a few families or else the community at large. Ample quantities of soup were made from plantains, peach-palm fruit or manioc. In each case the produce was cooked in pots, then mashed, mixed with water and poured into a canoe-like trough, from which each individual would scoop it into his own gourd bowl to offer it to other guests. Soup parties of this type could last for anything from just a few hours, if the guests were close neighbours, to as long as three or four days.

The first such party I attended was a fairly impromptu affair at a yano an hour's walk from Toototobi. After the invitation had been delivered, the guests paused only to paint themselves and each other carefully and to decorate their faces and arms with feathers, then set off cheerfully, walking in single file down a narrow forest path. Everyone carried his or her own gourd. The small boys larked about in excitement, pushing each other off the path, whistling to imitate birds and clapping in unison. Helio, as usual more elegantly painted than the rest, grabbed a palm leaf in passing and, within minutes, wove it into an extravagant headdress with trailing fronds.

After entering the host yano, our group headed immediately for the soup trough, which was half-full of warm, steaming plantain soup. They dipped their gourds repeatedly into the sweet, bland brew, giving each other huge draughts and smacking their lips. A real party atmosphere developed almost at once. Men stood together, forcing soup down one another's throats, laughing uproariously, exchanging ribald remarks and protesting from the very outset that they had already had too much to drink. Most of the women sat

Jocularly sporting a Brazilian farmworker's wicker hat he has obtained through trade, a man attending a party at a neighbouring yano rests against one of the support poles. Their frequent feasts provide opportunities for the Yanomami to indulge their sense of humour by dressing up in eccentric outfits, from a comical hat to a film of mud smeared over the body in imitation of wild pigs.

and watched more demurely, though a few joined in the fun. Only the previously noisy and bumptious children were subdued.

There were quiet interludes in the festivities during which everyone sat down to rest. Then the revelry would start up again, becoming riotous when some of the men managed to make themselves vomit the fresh, undigested juice, either by poking a leaf down their throats or else through simple over-indulgence. Everyone was delighted when this happened—the guests because it showed that they were being hospitably treated, the hosts because it demonstrated the lavishness of their generosity.

As time passed, the jokes became increasingly risqué, and much was made of the supposedly aphrodisiac effects of the soup. Victor and I were both reminded of stock party characters we knew from home as the party atmosphere led people to exaggerate their behaviour. We spotted the comedian, the very life and soul of the gathering, who made more fuss than anyone else when another drink was pressed on him, but downed it with gusto nonetheless; the shy, quiet type who sparkled as he emerged from his shell; the belle who politely accepted a drink from everyone but, secure in her attractiveness, needed do nothing more to win attention; the nice man who was always ready to talk to anyone who seemed out of things. All were there, behaving just like their counterparts at parties in Europe. The process of having a good time, we concluded, is extraordinarily universal.

At full swing, the pressure on each guest to drink more and yet more became intense. Their stomachs bulging, men staggered as though drunk, despite the fact that the soup contained no alcohol. Sometimes a whole chain of drinkers would form, each man forcing his gourd bowl on another and refusing to take no for an answer. This continued for three or four hours until all the soup was finished; and then, somewhat the worse for wear, our party wove an unsteady course home.

Impromptu soup parties provide one of the main activities of the Yanomami at the end of the dry season. Totting up the number of gatherings held in the month of April alone, I calculated that the Toototobi community attended nine such reunions at four separate sites, the farthest three days' walk away, and played host themselves on two occasions. It was, of course, an exceptional period, the high point of the Yanomami social year, and at any other time visits would have been less frequent. Even so, the constant coming and going indicated the developed network of communications between yanos spaced within walking distance of one another, and explained how it is that news can travel with surprising speed across the Yanomami homeland.

Yet for all their good-natured revelry, such small-scale gatherings cannot compare in scope or content with a full-scale funerary feast, the most elaborate of all Yanomami ceremonial occasions. A funerary feast, at which a dead person is mourned and the ashes disposed of, lasts for as long as a week. In preparation, the men of the host yano will for once hunt together, travelling far from the yano and living for several days in a camp set up in an area where the wild life is normally undisturbed, so as to be sure of providing an

impressive quantity of meat for their guests. Bunches of plantain will also be collected in advance and left to ripen, and the yano itself will be swept clean and its roof repaired if necessary.

Such feasts take their significance from the Yanomami attitude to death. The Yanomami believe that the only way to stop a dead person's soul from returning to life as an unhappy ghost is to remove totally every trace of his or her mortal existence. Dead bodies are invariably burnt, and the ashes of the bodies are preserved, often for many months, until they too can be disposed of in a suitably ceremonial manner.

The exact form of the funeral varies from one area of the Yanomami home-land to another. The Yanomamo-speakers, for instance, cremate their dead immediately after death. When someone dies in a Yanomam-speaking com-munity such as Toototobi, however, the corpse is left in the yano for a day, during which time there is universal weeping and lamentation. The body is then taken out into the forest, where it is wrapped tightly in a foetal position, and tied inside a bundle of sticks that serves to deter predators. The bundle is then bound with liana or wedged by means of poles against a tree trunk about six feet above the ground, and left to decompose. Only after several weeks is the skeleton taken down, then washed, stripped of any remaining flesh, and brought back to the centre of the yano, where it is burnt on a pyre. The ashes are then collected in a calabash, and preserved until arrangements

**Followed by his dog en route to a party at a neighbouring yano, Mateus uses the only boat his community possesses to transport two women with their babies across the Toototobi river. He has adorned himself with brilliant sprays of macaw feathers and has wrapped a sloth skin around his head.**

can be made for a funerary feast. At the feast, the Indians mix the ashes into plantain soup and swallow them.

Along with the ashes, every trace of the dead person's past life must be destroyed. Every possession that will burn is incinerated; unbreakable goods such as axes and hoes are thrown in the river. The individual's patches in the gardens are cut down and allowed to revert to forest. Even the earth floor of his hearth is raked over. All reference to him is avoided after his death, and his name is never spoken again.

The symbolic importance of a funerary feast is, then, to remove the last traces of the dead person with all due ceremony. At the same time, the attendant festivities enable the host yano to keep its alliances in good order by a display of generosity and the opportunity provided to exchange goods.

In the course of my stay, I was fortunate enough to attend a full-scale funerary feast, which included a couple of soup parties in its course. It took place not at Toototobi but at the neighbouring, allied yano we referred to by the name of its headman, Fialho. The feast was held to honour the ashes of an old woman who had died about a year before, and was attended by a large party of guests from a third yano, three days' walk away. They were present because the woman had at one time married into their community.

We arrived late on the day before the start of the feast, and found preparations already well under way. The following morning, Fialho—a skinny, wizened man in his middle years—encouraged everyone to speed up the preparation of the food in readiness for the guests. Soon afterwards, most of the young men left to do some last-minute hunting. The game that had already been collected during the previous week was moved and hung over the hearth of the keeper of the ashes who, we learnt, was the son of the old woman to whose memory the feast was dedicated.

In due course the three of us were roped in to help weed the plaza, while the young men of the yano cooked plantains over the fire beside the ceremonial soup trough. We worked hard, sweeping rubbish and loose earth into loads which could be carried outside for dumping. By the time the job was finished, the yano was immaculate and the whole great floor of beaten earth was as clean as a parade ground.

It was the middle of the morning when two hunters ran into the yano to announce that they had seen the visitors approaching. At once excitement spread to every hearth, and everyone began to paint and decorate themselves and their friends in all their finery to receive the guests. Fialho exhorted them to make themselves beautiful. "Even you ugly old women could do something to improve your looks, like putting dye on your noses," he said.

Suddenly the first of the visitors was among us. He came as a herald to announce the imminent arrival of the others. Beautifully painted with *urucu* and sporting two iridescent blue feathers in his ears, he came into the yano at a run, completing his entrance with a ballet-dancer's leap that brought him to a motionless halt. Having attracted universal attention, he walked over to Fialho and began to converse with the headman in one of the formal lan-

Returning to her yano after a successful foray to harvest peach-palm fruit for a feast, a woman crosses the flooded Toototobi river over a tree-trunk bridge with a handrail made of entwined lianas (above). Other members of the expedition (right), fording the river elsewhere, wade part of the way across and then climb on to a semi-submerged tree trunk to return to dry land.

guages reserved for such occasions, the disjointed, rhythmic drone used for Invitation Talk. As the two exchanged phrases, the newcomer remained standing, swinging his bow in a flamboyant arc at the end of each phrase.

Once the opening formalities had been completed, the messenger sat by himself for a time in the centre of the plaza, apparently deep in thought. He was given a calabash of plantain soup, which he drank while the men of the yano prepared a huge basket of smoked meat and manioc bread. Accepting this as a gift to be shared with his fellows, he left the yano to rejoin the rest of his party, who were waiting in a clearing outside to make a formal entrance.

The tension mounted after his departure as the hosts waited impatiently for the arrival of their guests. After a time shouts were heard, then suddenly the first of the visitors made their entrance. They were Yanomamo-dialect Indians—the group known to the Toototobi community as *shamatari*—who came from a yano on the Demini river, 30 miles or more to the west. In the manner of frontier dwellers all over the world, our hosts regarded these western neighbours, who spoke and acted rather differently from them, with a certain amount of suspicion, and a note of tension added spice to the first hours of the encounter between the two groups.

At first, single men, painted black and carrying axes or bows and arrows, rushed into the yano very fast, as though they had been running a great distance. Some were followed by small retinues of boys or girls, the boys carrying miniature bows and arrows, the girls bearing yellow palm fronds. They danced round the yano perimeter one by one, waving their weapons. This was the Presentation Dance, by which the visitors introduced themselves to the host community. Each man tried to particularize himself in some way, a few by the eccentricity of their decoration, others by adding a touch of humour to their performance. Most, however, chose to stress their elegance or valour. To this end, some chose to impersonate the spirits of animals renowned for their agility or courage, like the monkey or the jaguar. Meanwhile, the host party of men and boys formed a tight-knit group in the centre of the plaza, waving their arrows and axes as though to indicate that, however courageous their visitors might be, they would find the yano's own inhabitants ready to defend themselves.

After each individual had presented himself to his hosts, he left the yano. Eventually no more volunteers presented themselves, and for a moment the plaza stood empty of guests. Suddenly all the visitors entered as a group. They ran round the building and then gathered in its centre, stamping their feet and chanting faster and faster until the pace became quite frenzied. Without warning, they suddenly all stopped and stood motionless and impassive. The Presentation Dance was at an end.

Fialho and one or two of the older men indicated to the guests where they would be staying for the feast's duration. The women, who had for the most part been sitting in a quiet group by the entrance during the dancing, got up and joined their men at the various hearths to which they had been directed.

The remaining hours of daylight were taken up by a soup party, which served to put the guests rather more at their ease. That evening, Fialho, in his

## A Saturnalia of Soup

At times of the year when travel through the forest is easy and food is abundant, the Yanomami delight in giving parties for their neighbours in nearby yanos. At the feasts, which may last for a few hours or several days, huge quantities of soup, made from plantains, sweet manioc or peach-palm fruit, are consumed by the assembled party-goers.

Before the festivities, messengers are sent out bearing invitations to the guests. The hosts meanwhile collect the necessary foodstuffs from their gardens and bring them back to the yano, where the young men cook the comestibles and mix them with water to make the soup. On the day of the feast itself, the hosts and guests alike, spectacularly adorned with *urucu* dye and feather decorations, use their own gourds to scoop the soup out of a communal wood trough, cordially offering the bowls to one another. As the party goes on, the revellers are swept up by the festive spirit, and an air of exhilaration prevails.

Nevertheless, an undercurrent of aggression flows beneath the exaggerated generosity of the hosts and the affability of the guests. Men will encourage each other to drink more and more, forcing fresh bowls of soup on their victims until they are ready to vomit. Yet the implied hostility is sublimated in the prevailing atmosphere of good fellowship, and every excess is normally accepted with high spirits and laughter.

Looking weary and bloated from drinking too much plantain soup, Filipe, one of the hosts of a feast held in a yano near Toototobi, leans for support against a sturdy pole after emptying his gourd bowl. The need to consume food surpluses in the short period before they rot encourages party-goers to over-indulge in the sweet-tasting gruel.

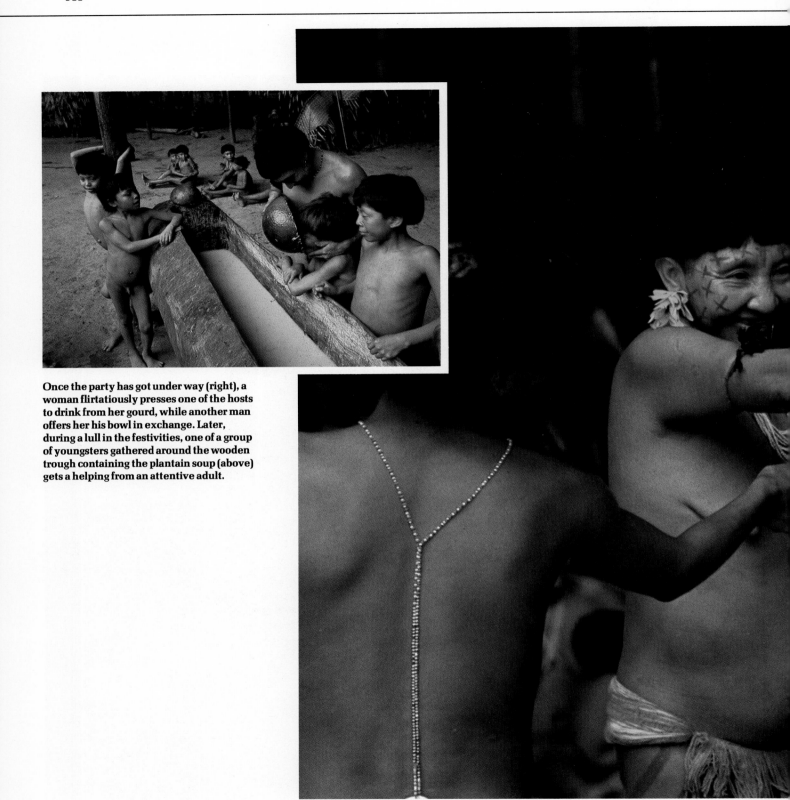

Once the party has got under way (right), a woman flirtatiously presses one of the hosts to drink from her gourd, while another man offers her his bowl in exchange. Later, during a lull in the festivities, one of a group of youngsters gathered around the wooden trough containing the plantain soup (above) gets a helping from an attentive adult.

His gourd empty, a tired but euphoric guest rests on his haunches to recover from the quantity of soup he has consumed. Many of those who over-indulge make themselves vomit so they can resume feasting.

role as headman, urged the young men to take part in News Talk. This formalized exchange of information is a traditional part of meetings between different Yanomami groups, and usually takes place through the night following the arrival of visitors. News concerning such topics as trading plans, visits, deaths, sorcery and love affairs is delivered in a series of drawn-out phrases, each ending on a sustained falling note. Working in relay with the other members of his party, each male guest took his turn at the chanting, while a member of the host yano stood opposite, commenting briefly on the news in counterpoint and then delivering stories of his own. While chanting, the men clutched their bows and arrows and stepped briskly from side to side, reaching down to touch the ground at the end of each phrase. So elaborate are the rhetorical circumlocutions and repetitions used on such occasions that News Talk invariably lasts well into the night. On this occasion it continued until the early dawn; I heard its rhythms echoing around the plaza as I drifted in and out of sleep in my hammock.

The next day was spent collecting manioc from the bereaved son's garden. He had reserved about a third of an acre as a special crop to be used for the feast, and from it perhaps a ton of tubers was collected. Nearly all the men joined in the labour, hosts and guests working together through the day. The women carried the tubers back to the yano.

That evening, the men and boys pulped some of the manioc to make a soup. Split and peeled chunks of tuber were boiled to soften them, and mashed in a small trough with a large wooden pestle. The purée was formed into balls; the balls were forced through wide-meshed liana baskets into the main soup trough, which had been filled, by my reckoning, with almost 100 gallons of water. During the night the cloudy liquid fermented slightly, making the surface frothy; the Yanomami say that the froth on the soup is caused by the anger of the men who do the mixing.

At about eight o'clock that evening, after darkness had fallen, Fialho encouraged the women to sing. At first the only response to his suggestion was laughter and joking, but after a time a soprano timidly struck up on the far side of the yano with a quavering song. After further exhortations from Fialho, an older woman began to chant, and the youngsters gradually joined in as a discordant chorus. At the same time one of Fialho's two wives began to dance, shuffling up and down on the edge of the plaza. Gradually, with much giggling, other women and girls joined her in an improvised chorus line. The rhythm of the chant was complicated, but the group gradually built up efficiency and enthusiasm, moving in a repeated pattern, four steps forward and three steps back, until they had made several circuits of the plaza.

The night was pitch dark and the only light to illuminate the dancers came from the fires glowing in every occupied hearth. It was well after midnight when the dancing finally came to an end and the women made their way back to their respective hearths. Even then silence did not fall, for soon afterwards a shaman began chanting to summon his spirit helpers.

The task of converting the manioc tubers into a huge quantity of bread, for distribution at the feast's end, occupied the next three days, which were also enlivened by a second soup party. Meanwhile, the game that had been smoking throughout the feast was cut up and boiled to provide food for the final day and to leave a surplus that could be distributed, along with the bread, among the guests before their departure.

On the fifth night—the last of the feast—the peace of the yano was disturbed from time to time by sounds of crying and wailing. The moment for the last rites was approaching, and the dead woman's close kin were starting the ritual mourning. The lamentations increased in volume after the sun had risen the next morning, when the bereaved son took down the gourd containing the ashes and poured them into a pot of plantain soup. The entire community, guests and hosts alike, gathered round the pot, amid universal weeping, while the liquid was drunk by some of the men present. The close kin were at the centre of the scene, but they did not drink the soup containing the ashes; were they to do so, according to Yanomam beliefs, their teeth would fall out and their innards would rot.

After every drop of the soup had been swallowed, the gourd in which the ashes had been preserved was broken into pieces and burnt, and the few remaining possessions of the dead woman were destroyed. At that moment a man carrying a clay disc made his way to the centre of the yano. On the plate was a heap of powdered *yakoana*, the hallucinogen that the Yanomami obtain from the bark of the *virola* tree. The man at once became the focus of attention as first the younger males and then all the menfolk surrounded him, gesticulating and shouting excitedly. Sitting on their haunches, the men began to inhale the hallucinogenic powder, at first in small quantities pinched between their fingers. Soon, however, hollow cane tubes were produced and, with the tubes criss-crossed over one another in an elaborate lattice and clouds of powder rising into the air, individuals started to blow the drug into one another's nostrils.

Within minutes, the scene was all confusion. Unaccustomed to the sensations produced by the drug, some of the young men sank to their knees and crawled along the ground or ran wildly around the yano, crying in terror. Older men more experienced with the hallucinogen pounded their chests as a sign of valour or grasped one another round the neck, addressing their partners in loud, exalted phrases. Shamans chanted and danced to summon their *hekura*. Amid the pandemonium, only the women—who never take the drug—remained passive at a safe distance, having taken care to store away any of their possessions that could be broken during the mêlée.

Rapidly, some sort of order began to reassert itself. While the adolescents sat against poles, gazing sightlessly into the distance as they sought to come to terms with the unfamiliar experiences they were undergoing, the older men began to pair off. Each man sank to his haunches with an arm around his partner's neck, to engage in the ceremonial dialogue known as Trade Talk. Chanting to a triple or quadruple beat, the men started by exchanging declarations of friendship and offers of barter. As the dialogues progressed, however, some of the couples passed from good will to grievances, and noisily accused each other of everything from impoliteness in refusing proffered food to competition for a girl's favours. As their passions mounted, each partner's grip on the other's neck tightened until sweat ran down their foreheads. One pair of men started rolling on the ground, slapping at each other with their free hands. The rest of the gathering remained unresponsive, however, and in time the tempers of the aggrieved men cooled and harmony was restored. Rising to their feet, the fighters made their way to the river to wash off the dust they had picked up from the yano's floor.

Meanwhile, huge piles of boiled meat and manioc bread were being assembled on a carpet of palm leaves in the centre of the plaza. The elders of the host yano discussed in low voices how to apportion the food before dispatching younger men with laden baskets for each of the guest families. When all the guests had received their shares, the remainder of the food was distributed among the hosts.

After the division of the food, trading began between individuals around the yano. Arrows, bows, gourds of *urucu* dye, hammocks and earthenware plates were swapped for machetes, knives, axes and aluminium cooking pots in intense and protracted negotiations that, however, always ended with deals being made; for to refuse a proferred exchange outright would be considered openly insulting. Then the headmen of the two communities got together to discuss plans for future feasts. Once suitable arrangements had been made, the guests got ready to leave. The women were the first to go, and one by one the men followed them, departing in typical Yanomami fashion with no word or gesture of farewell other than a laconic "I'm going home". Suddenly the yano, which had been so full and animated for the past week, seemed empty and silent. Only the sound of a girl crying by her hearth for a departed lover broke the stillness. Thereafter the yano returned once more to its peaceful daily routine.

Lying in my hammock back at Toototobi after the feast as the women gossiped cheerfully and a group of small boys sat talking and joking with Bruce about the outside world, I found it hard to imagine how the way of life of the Yanomami could be improved. The overriding sensation I felt was one of security. We were in the midst of a community of about 100 people, all of whom knew and acknowledged us, responding readily with a grin when we smiled. The people were so kind, tolerant and genuinely friendly that it was hard to think that, when an Asa de Socorro plane airlifted me back to Boa Vista and the modern world the following day, I might have seen the last of a society that, without intelligent and tactful handling on the part of the responsible authorities, may soon disappear for ever.

For the Yanomami lifestyle, which I had learnt to respect and admire, is now under threat. Modern communications are impinging on the isolation that has kept their customs intact and inviolate for thousands or even tens of thousands of years. The most immediate menace to the Yanomami has been the projected routing of a highway—the *Perimetral Norte*, or Northern Perimeter of the Trans-Amazonian road system—through some 400 miles of their homeland. The road was originally intended as a central part of a huge

Women carrying baskets of manioc (inset) make their way through a garden back to the yano, where the tubers will be prepared for a feast. Inside the building, a temporary silo is constructed from poles and banana leaves to hold the manioc until the time comes to grate it and use it to make bread.

development scheme that would, if implemented, have led to extensive economic exploitation of much of the eastern part of the Indians' territory, from Boa Vista almost to Toototobi.

At the time of writing, however, construction of the road has mercifully been stopped, for want of funds. The decision came too late to save some fringe Yanomami groups, who have suffered disastrously from the 130 miles of roadway that have already been built. The bulldozers passed within 100 yards of certain yanos, knocking down gardens and peach-palm groves on their way. In all, about a dozen yanos disappeared as a result of the project, and many of their inhabitants died. I saw some of the survivors for myself on the road before I went to Toototobi. Ragged and poor, they stood begging by the roadside. They lived in scattered encampments next to equally poor Brazilian settlers, who had moved as far up the road as the government would allow in search of lands to farm.

Even if the *Perimetral Norte* is never completed, however, the tribe will have been granted little more than a temporary reprieve. By radio and aeroplane the modern world will still find a way into the remote forest fastnesses that have sheltered them for so long. Unless prevenmive measures are taken, it will inevitably bring in its wake more epidemic diseases and economic dependency. Worse still, the Indians may, in spite of all their pride and resilience, come to doubt the worth of their own culture and way of life. In the face of a more powerful technology, they may decline into beggary of the type I had already seen along the roadway's route and in so many places elsewhere in the world. Such a process would benefit no one—neither the intruders, who would be left with another social burden on their hands, nor the Indians, who would be destroyed.

Fortunately, another, happier alternative does exist, and its outlines are already becoming clear. The Brazilian government has recently approved in principle plans for the establishment of a Yanomami national park, to be administered under the aegis of FUNAI, the Brazilian governmental agency responsible for Indian affairs. The purpose of such a park would be to provide the territorial security and protection of natural resources that are essential if the Yanomami are to continue as an economically independent society able to preserve its own cultural values. In time, if the project is put into law, they might develop ways to remain self-supporting even if trading links with the outside world continue. They would thereby be saved from selling their labour, an arrangement that in the past has invariably led Indians to enter industrial society as an exploited workforce, fit only for the most menial jobs.

To achieve this goal, they must retain their homeland intact. The region surrounding the Parima Massif is the land of their ancestors, where all their history and their myths are based. To remove any part of it would be to destroy the tribe's roots and all their cultural reference points, and this would be as great a blasphemy in Yanomami eyes as the mass destruction of the cathedrals of Europe would appear to us.

The setting up of such a park, guaranteeing the Indians' right to the land in perpetuity, is a prerequisite if the Yanomami are to be saved. It would in itself, however, be only the first step in a continuing process of survival. A heavy responsibility would still rest on the administrators of the park to protect the interests of the Indians within its bounds. They would have to show concern not only for the material well-being of the Yanomami but also for their culture, and in particular for shamanism as the bedrock of the tribe's social life. Another essential would be an effective medical service to protect the Indians from epidemic diseases. The doctors providing the service could gain from the Indians as much as they gave them, because they would have a unique opportunity to learn about the Indians' use of medicinal plants.

If such measures are taken in time, there is no reason why the Yanomami should not adapt, survive and even flourish. The Indians are already preparing themselves intellectually for a new relationship with outsiders. One of their myths tells the familiar tale of a great flood—in this case, one that swept away the people of a yano that had failed to observe essential rituals. In the water, the victims were attacked and torn apart by giant otters and black caymans. The blood-stained foam was washed ashore on a beach at the world's end, where Bumblebee, the mythical ancestor of all the bee tribe, lived. Bumblebee brought the pink foam to his mouth and whispered over it, and from this act, the shamans say, foreigners were born.

The Yanomami have long used this story to explain the strange, unstressed speech pattern of the outsiders with whom they have had contact, which to their ears sounds like the buzzing of bees. Indeed, small boys used to tease Victor and me by imitating the sound behind our backs when we first arrived at Toototobi. Now, however, the Indians give it a new interpretation. The story shows, they say, that all foreigners are simply Yanomami who have been transformed, and the mighty products of their technology merely the generous gifts of Bumblebee, the spirit that gave them birth. But, the Indians add, he expected the people he created to show equal generosity to those from whose blood they sprang. This dignified interpretation of their relationship with the outside world encourages the Yanomami to expect fair treatment as a right. One can only hope that they will not be disappointed.

# A Grand Farewell to the Dead

The most elaborate of all Yanomami social gatherings are funerary feasts held to dispose of the ashes of the dead. Custom demands that after death all memory of a person must be erased. The feasts provide an opportunity to perform the last rites ceremonially, in the presence of grieving relatives.

Such feasts, which last for about a week, require careful planning. First the host yano's menfolk take part in a communal hunt to provide game. Messengers are then dispatched to invite friends and relatives of the dead person from neighbouring yanos. On their return, additional food is gathered from the gardens. At the appointed time, the guests travel to the

Before a funerary feast at a yano near Toototobi, the chief host turns the ribs of a wild pig on a rack over a fire so they will cure evenly before being

vicinity of the yano, where they pause to decorate themselves. A herald is sent to announce their arrival, then they make a spectacular entrance, engaging first individually then together in a dance of presentation.

The next few days are given over to socializing, until the time comes, on the last day of the feast, for the disposal of the ashes—either by drinking them in soup or burying them in the yano floor. Afterwards, the men take hallucinogens and enter animated dialogues about the exchange of goods. Thereafter the mood lightens, and the celebrations come to an end with the distribution of manioc bread and smoked meats to the departing guests.

boiled. As nearest relative of the deceased—in this case a woman—he supervises the preparation of food and takes charge of the dead person's ashes.

At the start of the feast, a herald from the guest party engages the headman of the host yano in the customary embrace used for Invitation Talk, a formal

exchange of greetings and information. The herald's head is covered with bird down, traditionally worn by guests; bright blue feathers adorn his ears.

While the guests approach the yano, some of the hosts move into the centre of the building to give a ritual display of strength (right), waving bows, arrows, sticks and hatchets in the air. On arrival, the guests introduce themselves with a dance of presentation. One participant (above), his body decorated with charcoal and bird feathers, acts the part of a capuchin monkey—considered to be agile and quick-witted, attributes of a good warrior.

A few days before the conclusion of the feast, women—hosts and guests alike—grate manioc on to a work surface of bark stripped from a single tree. The grated manioc is made into bread to be distributed to the guests on the last day of the festivities.

Late at night, a group of women and young girls join in line for an improvised dance, performed to a succession of short songs, in the yano's central plaza. Such impromptu celebrations may take place any evening during the feast when the participants feel inspired to celebrate the abundance of food.

On the feast's last day, the ashes of the dead woman are emptied from the small gourd in which they have been preserved into a pot of plantain soup. The soup is offered only to certain men not closely related to the dead person. Other relations—among them a weeping woman (below)—sit nearby, mourning their departed kinswoman.

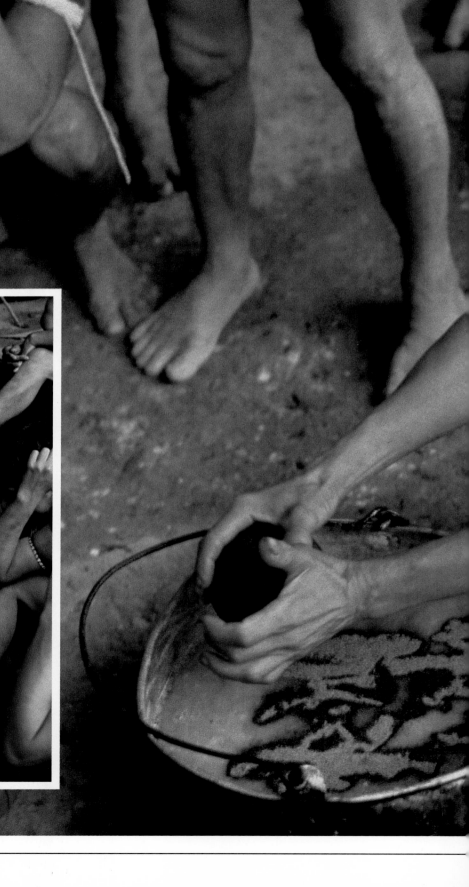

Towards the end of the feast, two men sit hugging each other in the customary posture adopted for Trade Talk, a ritualized discussion between hosts and guests about goods they wish to exchange. The parley is usually preceded by the inhalation of hallucinogens and the dialogues sometimes turn into an exchange of grievances that can end in blows. In one such case (inset), an angry woman protects her husband by threatening his partner with a knife and a machete.

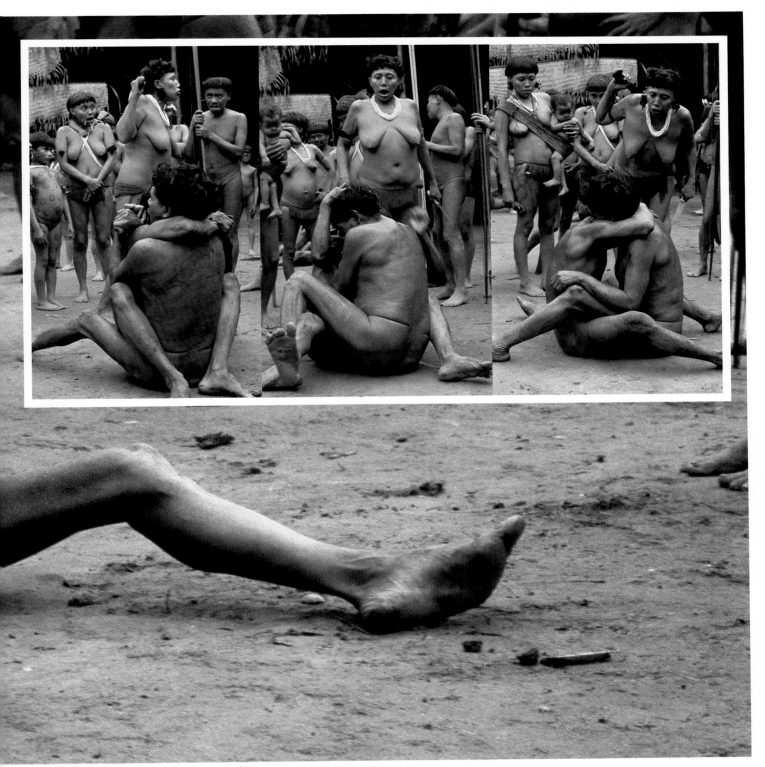

# Bibliography

Albert, Bruce, "Yanomami—Kaingang: la Question des Terres Indiennes au Brésil", in *Indianité, Ethnocide, Indigènisme en Amérique Latine*, ed. F. Morin. Éditions du Centre National de la Recherche Scientifique, Paris, 1982.

Albert, B., and Carlo Zacquini, "Yanomami Indian Park, Proposal and Justification", in *Yanoama in Brazil 1979*, ed. A. Ramos and K. Taylor. ARC/IWGIA/SI Document no. 37, Copenhagen, 1979.

Biocca, Ettore, *Yanoama, the Story of a Woman Abducted by Brazilian Indians*. George Allen and Unwin, London, 1969.

Bourne, Richard, *Assault on the Amazon*. Victor Gollancz, London, 1978.

Chagnon, Napoleon A., *Yanomamo: The Fierce People*. Holt, Rinehart & Winston, New York, 1968.

Chagnon, Napoleon A., P. Lequesne and J. U. Cook, "Yanomamo Hallucinogens: Anthropological, Botanical and Chemical Findings", in *Current Anthropology*, 12(1), 1971.

Chagnon, Napoleon A., *Studying the Yanomamo*. Holt, Rinehart & Winston, New York, 1974.

Clastres, H., and J. Lizot, "La Part du Feu, Rites et Discours de la Mort chez les Yanomami", *Libre 3*, Payot, Paris, 1978.

Coco, L., *Iyewei-teri. Quince anos entre los Yanomamos*. Escuela Tecnica popular Don Bosco, Caracas.

Davis, S., *Victims of the Miracle: Development and the Indians of Brazil*. Cambridge University Press, 1977.

Davis S., "The Yanomamo: Ethnographic Images and Anthropological Responsibilities", in *The Geological Imperative* by Shelton Davis and Robert Mathews. Anthropology Resource Center, Cambridge, Massachusetts, 1976.

Denevan, W., "The Aboriginal Population of Amazonia", in *The Native Population of the Americas in 1492*, ed. W. Denevan. University of Wisconsin Press, 1976.

Dostal, Professor Dr. W., ed., *The Situation of the Indian in South America*. Geneva, 1972.

Goodland, R. J. A., and H. S. Irwin, *Amazon Jungle: Green Hell to Red Desert*. Amsterdam, 1975.

Gross, D. R., ed., *Peoples and Cultures of Native South America*. Doubleday/Natural History Press for the American Museum of Natural History, 1973.

Hames, R., ed., "Game Depletion and Hunting Zone Rotation among the Ye'kwana and Yanomamo of Amazonas, Venezuela", in *Studies in Hunting and Fishing in the Neotropics*. Working papers on South American Indians, Bennington College, Vermont, 1980.

Hanbury-Tenison, Robin, *A Question of Survival*. Angus & Robertson, London, 1973.

Hemming, J., *Red Gold: the Conquest of the Brazilian Indians*. Macmillan, London, 1978.

Koch-Grunberg, T., *Vom Roroima zum Orinoco*. Dietrich Reimer (Ernst Vohsen), Berlin, 1917.

Lathrap, D., *The Upper Amazon*. Thames and Hudson, London, 1970.

Lizot, J., "Economie ou Société? Quelques Thèmes à propos d'une Communauté d'Amerindians", in *Journal de la Société des Americanistes*, vol. LX, Paris, 1971.

Lizot, J., "Poisons Yanomami de Chasse, de Guerre et de Pêche", in *Antropológica 31*, Venezuela, 1972.

Lizot, J., *Le Cercle des Feux: Faits et Dits des Indiens Yanomami*. Éditions du Seuil, Paris, 1976.

Lizot, J., *The Yanomami in the Face of Ethnocide*. IWGIA, Copenhagen, 1976.

Lizot, J., "Population, Resources and Warfare among the Yanomami", in *Man* (N.S.)12, 1977.

Lizot, J., "Economie Primitive et Subsistance. Essai sur le Travail et l'Alimentation chez les Yanomami", *Libre 4*, Payot, Paris, 1978.

Lizot, J., "Connaissance et Usage des Plantes Sauvages chez les Yanomami", in *Unidad y variedad*, IVIC, Caracas, 1978.

Lyon, P., ed., *Native South Americans*. Little Brown, Boston, Toronto, 1974.

Meggers, Betty, *Amazonia: Man and Culture in a Counterfeit Paradise*, Chicago, 1971.

Migliazza, E., *Yanomama Grammar and Intelligibility*, Ph.D. thesis, University of Indiana, 1972.

Moerman, D. E., "Anthropology of Symbolic Healing", in *Current Anthropology*, vol. 20, no. 1, 1979.

Neel, J. V., "Genetic Aspects of the Ecology of Disease in the American Indian", in *The Ongoing Evolution of the Latin American Population*, ed. F. A. Salzano. C. C. Thomas, Springfield, Illinois, 1971.

Neel, J. V., "Health and Disease in an Unacculturated Amerindian Population", in *Health and Disease in Tribal Societies*, Ciba Foundation Symposium 49 (New Series) Elsevier/Excerpta Medica/North Holland and Elsevier North Holland, Inc., 1977.

Neel, J. V., et al., "Notes on the Effect of Measles and Measles Vaccine in a Virgin-Soil Population of South American Indians," in *American Journal of Epidemiology*, vol. 91, 1970.

Neel, J. V., et al., "Studies on the Yanomama Indians", in *Proceedings of the 4th International Congress of Human Genetics*, Excerpta Medica, Amsterdam, 1972.

Prance, G. T., "Notes on the Use of Plant Hallucinogens in Amazonian Brazil", *Economic Botany*, 24(1), 1970.

Prance, G. T., "Ethnobotanical Notes from Amazonian Brazil", *Economic Botany*, 26(3) 1973.

Prance, G. T., "An Ethnobotanical Comparison of Four Tribes of Amazonian Indians", *Acta Amazonica*, 2 (2), 1973.

Prance, G. T., "The Origin and Evolution of the Amazon Flora", *Interciencia* 3 (4), 1978.

Ramos, A., and B. Albert, "Yanoama Descent and Affinity: The Sanuma/Yanomam Contrast", *Actes du 42ème Congrès International des Americanistes*, Paris, 1977.

Ramos, A., "On Women's Status in Yanoama Societies", in *Current Anthropology*, vol. 20, no. 1, 1979.

Ramos, A., "Yanoama Indians in North Brazil Threatened by Highway", in *Yanoama in Brazil*, ed. A. Ramos and K. Taylor, 1979. ARC/IWGIA/SI Document no. 37, Copenhagen, 1979.

Ramos, A., *Hieraquia e Simbiose. Relações Intertribais no Brasil*. Editora Hucitec, São Paulo, 1980.

Rice, A. Hamilton, "The Rio Branco, Uraricuera and Parima", in *The Geographical Journal*, vol. 71, 1928.

Richards, P. W., *The Tropical Rainforest: An Ecological Study*. Cambridge University Press, 1966 (1952).

Schauensee, Rodolphe Meyer de, and William H. Phelps, Jnr., *A Guide to the Birds of Venezuela*. Princeton University Press, Princeton, 1978.

Schomburgk, R. H., "Report of the Third Expedition into the Interior of Guayana, 1837-1838", in *Journal of the R.G.S.*, 10, 1840.

Schultes, R. E., and Albert Hofmann, *Plants of the Gods*. Hutchinson, London, 1979.

Smole, W., *The Yanoama Indians: A Cultural Geography*. Austin, London, 1976.

Steward, J., *Handbook of the South American Indians*. 5 vols., Smithsonian Institute, Washington D.C., 1949/1950.

Taylor, K. I., *Sanuma Fauna: Prohibitions and Classifications*. Fund. La Salle de Ciencas Naturales, Caracas, 1974.

Taylor, K. I., "Body and Spirit among the Sanuma (Yanoama) of North Brazil", in *Medical Anthropology*, ed. F. X. Grollig and H. B. Haley. Mouton, 1976.

Taylor, K. I., "Development against the Yanoama: The Case of Mining and Agriculture", in *Yanoama in Brazil*, ed. A. Ramos and K. Taylor. ARC/IWGIA/SI Document no. 37, Copenhagen, 1979.

Zerries, O., and M. Schuster, *Waika & Mahekodotedi*. 2 vols., Kleis Renner Verlag, Munich, 1964 and 1974.

# Acknowledgements and Picture Credits

The author and editors of this book wish to thank the following: Claudia Andujar, Co-ordinator, Committee for the Creation of the Yanomami Park, São Paulo, Brazil; Asas de Socorro, Boa Vista, Brazil; Brazilian Embassy, London; British Museum (Natural History) Department of Library Services; Mike Brown; CNPQ (National Council for Scientific and Technological Research), Brasilia, Brazil; FUNAI (National Foundation of the Indians), Brasilia, Brazil; Dr. Conrad Gorinsky, St. Bartholomew's Medical College, London; Mary Harron; Library of the Museum of Man-kind, London; Library of the Royal Geographical Society, London; Ministry of External Relations, Brasilia, Brazil; Memelia Moreira; New Tribes Mission, Toototobi and Manaus, Brazil; Dr. Ghillean T. Prance, New York Botanical Garden; Royal Botanic Gardens, Kew, Richmond, Surrey; Dr. Richard Evan Schultes, Harvard Botanical Museum; Survival International, London.

The sources for the pictures in this book are listed on the right. Credits for each of the photographers and illustrators are listed by page numbers in sequence; where necessary, the locations of pictures within pages are also indicated—separated from page numbers by dashes.

All photographs by Victor Englebert except: Bruce Albert, 162-163, 164-165. Martha Englebert, 4—middle. Marika Hanbury-Tenison, 4—top. Timothy Luxton, 4—bottom. Dr. Ghillean Prance, 115. Paul Reeves, 115—top right. Illustrations (alphabetically): Maps by Terry Allen and Nicholas Skelton for Creative Cartography Ltd., 22-23. Front end-paper map by Engineering Surveys Reproduction Ltd. Shaman's drawing by Taniki, 121.

# Index

Colour separations by Scan Studios Ltd.—Dublin, Ireland.
Typesetting by G. Beard & Son, Ltd.—Brighton, England.
Printed and bound by Brepols S.A.—Turnhout, Belgium.